LESSON ONE

Nouns

Refers to one	وَاحِد	Refers to two/dual	تَثْنِيَه
A word that shows more than two	جَمْع	Masculine	مُذَكَّر
Refers to one	مُؤَنَّث		

Masculine Singular

Worshipper	عَابِدٌ	One who praises	حَامِدٌ
One who prostrates	سَاجِدٌ	One who is humble	خَاشِعٌ
One who is standing	قَائِمٌ	One performing Ruku`	رَاكِعٌ
One who is sitting	قَاعِدٌ		

Feminine Singular

Worshipper	عَابِدَةٌ	One who praises	حَامِدَةٌ
One who prostrates	سَاجِدَةٌ	One who is humble	خَاشِعَةٌ
One who is standing	قَائِمَةٌ	One performing Ruku`	رَاكِعَةٌ
One who is sitting	قَاعِدَةٌ		

Scale

	Masculine	Feminine
Singular	عَابِدٌ	عَابِدَةٌ
	He is worshipper	She is worshipper
Dual	عَابِدَانِ	عَابِدَتَانِ
	They are worshippers	They are worshippers
Plural	عَابِدُوْنَ	عَابِدَاتٌ
	They are worshippers	They are worshippers

Exercise

Translate the words below. Consider the singular, dual and plural forms as well as masculine and feminine:

They praise (dual masculine) حَامِدَانِ

They praise (dual feminine) حَامِدَتَانِ

They praise (plural masculine) حَامِدُوْنَ

They praise (plural feminine) حَامِدَاتٌ

They prostrate (dual masculine) سَاجِدَانِ

They prostrate (dual feminine) سَاجِدَاتَانِ

They prostrate (plural masculine) سَاجِدُوْنَ

They prostrate (plural feminine) سَاجِدَاتٌ

They are humble (dual masculine) خَاشِعَانِ

They are humble (dual feminine)	خَاشِعَتَانِ
They are humble (plural masculine)	خَاشِعُوْنَ
They are humble (plural feminine)	خَاشِعَاتٌ
They make ruku' (dual masculine)	رَاكِعَانِ
They make ruku' (dual feminine)	رَاكِعَتَانِ
They make ruku' (plural masculine)	رَاكِعُوْنَ
They make ruku' (plural feminine)	رَاكِعَاتٌ
They worship (plural masculine)	عَابِدُوْنَ
They are standing (plural masculine)	قَائِمُوْنَ
They are sitting (plural masculine)	قَاعِدُوْنَ
They are prostrating (plural masculine)	سَاجِدُوْنَ
They are worshippers (plural feminine)	عَابِدَاتٌ
They are standing (plural feminine)	قَائِمَاتٌ
They are making ruku'(plural feminine)	رَاكِعَاتٌ
They are prostrating (plural feminine)	سَاجِدَاتٌ

LESSON TWO

Indicative nouns

	Masculine	**Feminine**
Singular	هٰذَا ذٰلِكَ	هٰذِهِ تِلْكَ
	This, That	This, That
Dual	هٰذَانِ	هَاتَانِ
	These two men	These two women
Plural	هٰؤُلَاءِ أُولٰئِكَ	هٰؤُلَاءِ أُولٰئِكَ
	These men	These women

Indicative nouns

The person or thing which is being indicated towards is called Mushaarun Ilayh. When the noun of Ishaara comes with the Mushaarun Ilayh, Alif Laam will come on the Mushaarun Ilayh. For e.g. (هٰذَا النَّبِيُّ) This Nabi. (هٰذَا) Is the noun of Ishaara and (اَلنَّبِيُّ) is the Mushaarun Ilayh.

Rasul	اَلرَّسُوْلُ	Town, Village	اَلْقَرْيَةُ
Book	اَلْكِتَابُ	Tree	اَلشَّجَرَةُ
Qur`aan	اَلْقُرْاٰنُ	Jannah	اَلْجَنَّةُ
House	اَلْبَيْتُ	Hell	اَلنَّارُ
City	اَلْبَلَدُ	Day	اَلْيَوْمُ

Night	اَللَّيْلَةُ	Springs	اَلْأَنْهَارُ
Man	اَلرَّجُلُ	Speech	اَلْحَدِيثُ
Woman	اَلْاِمْرَءَةُ	Life	اَلْحَيْوةُ
Boy	اَلْوَلَدُ	House	اَلدَّارُ
Girl	اَلْبِنْتُ		

Exercise

Taking into consideration the masculine, feminine, singular, dual and plural, whether close or far indication, translate:

This Rasul - هٰذَا الرَّسُوْلُ   This speech - هٰذَا الْحَدِيثُ

That book - ذٰلِكَ الْكِتَابُ   That boy - ذٰلِكَ الْوَلَدُ

This Qur`aan - هٰذَا الْقُرْآنُ   That girl - تِلْكَ الْبِنْتُ

This house - هٰذَا الْبَيْتُ   That religion - ذٰلِكَ الدَّيْنُ

This city - هٰذَا الْبَلَدُ   This life - هٰذِهِ الْحَيْوةُ

This town - هٰذَا الْقَرْيَةُ   That house - تِلْكَ الدَّارُ

That tree - تِلْكَ الشَّجَرَةُ   These two men - هٰذَانِ الرَّجُلَانِ

This Jannah - هٰذِهِ الْجَنَّةُ   Those two women - هَاتَانِ الْاِمْرَءَتَانِ

That fire - تِلْكَ النَّارُ   Those men - هٰؤُلَاءِ الرِّجَالُ

These springs - هٰذِهِ الْأَنْهَارُ   Those women - هٰؤُلَاءِ النِّسَاءُ

That day - ذٰلِكَ الْيَوْمُ   Those men - أُولٰئِكَ الرِّجَالُ

That night - تِلْكَ اللَّيْلَةُ   Those women - أُولٰئِكَ النِّسَاءُ

That man - ذٰلِكَ الرَّجُلُ

That woman - تِلْكَ الْاِمْرَءَةُ

LESSON THREE

Indicative noun and its subject

When the indicative noun indicates to some person or thing and give information about it, then the indicative noun will be mubtada and that news of it will be khabar. There is no Alif Laam brought on the khabar. For e.g. (هذا مؤمن) this is a believing man. (هذه مؤمنة) this is a believing woman, (ذلك مسلم) that is a Muslim man, (تلك مسلمة) that is a Muslim woman.

Path/Way	صِرَاطٌ	Palace	صَرْحٌ
Proof	حُجَّةٌ	Boulder	صَخْرَةٌ
Sin	إِثْمٌ	Two pious men	صَالِحَانِ
Group	أُمَّةٌ	Two proofs	بُرْهَانَانِ
Serpent	ثُعْبَانٌ	Two magicians	سَاحِرَانِ
Snake	حَيَّةٌ	People of Jannah	أَصْحَابُ الْجَنَّةِ
The group of Shaytaan	حِزْبُ الشَّيْطَانِ	People of fire	أَصْحَابُ النَّارِ
		The group of Allah	حِزْبُ اللهِ

this path   هٰذَا صِرَاطٌ

that proof   تِلْكَ حُجَّةٌ

that sin   ذَالِكَ إِثْمٌ

that nation   تِلْكَ أُمَّةٌ

this serpent   هٰذَا ثُعْبَانٌ

this snake   هٰذِهِ حَيَّةٌ

this palace   هٰذَا صَرْحٌ

This boulder	هٰذِهِ صَخْرَةٌ
These two proofs	هٰذَانِ بُرْهَانَانِ
These two magicians	هٰذَانِ سَاحِرَانِ
These two pious men	هٰذَانِ صَالِحَانِ
These are the people of Jannah	أُوْلٰئِكَ أَصْحَابُ الْجَنَّةِ
That is the group of Allah	أُوْلٰئِكَ حِزْبُ اللهِ
Those are the people of the fire	أُوْلٰئِكَ أَصْحَابُ النَّارِ
That is the group of Shaytaan	أُوْلٰئِكَ حِزْبُ الشَّيْطَانِ

LESSON FOUR

Mudaaf and Mudaaf Ilayh

The Mudaaf comes first, then the Mudaaf Ilayh. When translating, then the Mudaaf Ilayh is translated first, then the Mudaaf. In between will be the word 'of'. For e.g. (رسول الله) Rasul of Allaah. (كتاب الله) Book of Allaah, (ملائكة الله) angels of Allaah.

Name	اِسْمٌ	Morning	اَلْفَلَقِ
Rabb	رَبٌّ	Dark night	غَاسِقٍ
The universe	اَلْعَالَمِيْنَ	Those who blow	اَلنَّفَّاثَاتِ
Day	يَوْمٌ	Jealous	حَاسِدٍ
Recompense	اَلدِّيْنُ	Punishment	عَذَابٌ
People	اَلنَّاسِ	Fire	اَلنَّارُ
King	مَلِكٌ	Night	لَيْلَةٌ
Deity	إِلهٌ	Power	اَلْقَدْرُ
Evil	شَرٌّ	People, owner	أَصْحَابٌ
Deceiver	اَلْوِسْوَاسُ	Elephant	اَلْفِيْلُ
Chests	صُدُوْرٌ	Speech	حَدِيْثٌ
Qiyaamat	اَلْغَاشِيَةُ		

The name of Allaah	اِسْمُ اللهِ
Rabb of the universe	رَبِّ الْعَالَمِيْنَ
Day of recompense	يَوْمِ الدِّيْنِ
Rabb of the people	رَبِّ النَّاسِ

King of the people	مَلِكِ النَّاسِ
Deity of the people	اِلٰهِ النَّاسِ
Evil of the deceiver	شَرِّ الْوَسْوَاسِ
Chests of people	صُدُوْرِ النَّاسِ
Rabb of the Morning	رَبِّ الْفَلَقِ
Evil of the dark night	شَرِّ غَاسِقٍ
Evil of those who blow	شَرِّ النَّفَّاثَاتِ
Evil of the jealous	شَرِّ حَاسِدٍ
Punishment of the fire	عَذَابَ النَّارِ
Night of power	لَيْلَةُ الْقَدْرِ
People of the elephant	أَصْحَابِ الْفِيْلِ
Talk of Qiyaamat	حَدِيْثُ الْغَاشِيَةِ

LESSON FIVE

Mausoof and Sifat

The word whose good or evil is being explained is called Mausoof. The word showing the good or bad quality is called Sifat. The Mausoof comes first, then the Sifat. When translating, the Sifat is placed first, then the Mausoof. For e.g. (رسول كريم) Noble Rasul, (كتاب مرقوم) written book, (جنة عالية) high paradise.

Beneficent	اَلرَّحْمٰنُ	Tree	اَلشَّجَرِ
Merciful	اَلرَّحِيْم	Green	اَلْأَخْضَرِ
Shaytaan	اَلشَّيْطَان	Punishment	عَذَابٌ
Rejected	اَلرَّجِيْم	Painful	اَلِيْمٌ
Path	اَلصِّرَاط	Magician	سَاحِرٌ
Straight	اَلْمُسْتَقِيْم	Lying	كَذَّابٌ
Deceiver	اَلْوَسْوَاس	Slave	عَبْدٌ
Straw	عَصْفٍ	Believer	مُؤْمِنٌ
Eaten	مَأْكُوْلٍ	Female slave	اَمَةٌ
Success	اَلْفَوْزُ	Female believer	مُؤْمِنَةٌ
Great	اَلْعَظِيْمُ	Speech	كَلِمَةٌ
Spring	عَيْنٌ	Good	طَيِّبَةٌ
Flowing	جَارِيَةٌ	Evil	خَبِيْثَةٌ
Clear	مُبِيْنٌ	One who draws back	اَلْخَنَّاس

Allaah is Beneficent, Merciful	اَللهِ الرَّحْمٰنِ الرَّحِيْمِ
Rejected Shaytaan	اَلشَّيْطَانِ الرَّجِيْمِ
The straight path	اَلصِّرَاطَ الْمُسْتَقِيْمَ
The deception of the one who draws back	اَلْوَسْوَاسِ الْخَنَّاسِ
Eaten straw	عَصْفٍ مَّأْكُوْلٍ
Great success	اَلْفَوْزُ الْعَظِيْمُ
Flowing spring	عَيْنٌ جَارِيَةٌ
Clear book	كِتَابٌ مُبِيْنٌ
Green tree	اَلشَّجَرِ الْاَخْضَرِ
Painful punishment	عَذَابٌ اَلِيْمٌ
Lying magician	سَاحِرٌ كَذَّابٌ
Believing slave	عَبْدٌ مُؤْمِنٌ
Believing female slave	اَمَةٌ مُؤْمِنَةٌ
Good speech	كَلِمَةٍ طَيِّبَةٍ
Evil speech	كَلِمَةٍ خَبِيْثَةٍ
Good tree	شَجَرَةٍ طَيِّبَةٍ
Evil tree	شَجَرَةٍ خَبِيْثَةٍ

LESSON SIX

Pronoun (Dhameer)

Singular

هُوَ	هِیَ	اَنْتَ	اَنْتِ	اَنَا
He	She	You (m)	You (f)	I (m&f)

Dual

هُمَا	هُمَا	اَنْتُمَا	اَنْتُمَا	نَحْنُ
They (m)	They (f)	You two (m)	You two(f)	We (m&f)

Plural

هُمْ	هُنَّ	اَنْتُمْ	اَنْتَنَّ	نَحْنُ
They (m)	They (f)	You (m)	You (f)	We (m&f)

Exercise

One who is successful	فَائِزٌ
One who is at loss	خَاسِرٌ
One who worships	قَانِتٌ
ious	صَالِحٌ
One who advises	نَاصِحٌ
One who overpowers	غَالِبٌ
Writer	كَاتِبٌ

Oppressor	ظَالِمٌ
Successful	مُفْلِحٌ
Polytheist	مُشْرِكٌ
One who has conviction	مُوْقِنٌ
One who is grateful	شَاكِرٌ

Sentences

He is a worshipper	هُوَ قَانِتٌ
She is grateful	هِيَ شَاكِرَةٌ
They (dual) are pious	هُمَا صَالِحَانِ
They are successful	هُمْ فَائِزُوْنَ
She is an oppressor	هِيَ ظَالِمَةٌ
They (dual) are at loss	هُمَا خَاسِرَتَانِ
They are fasting	هُنَّ صَائِمَاتٌ
You (plural) are oppressors	أَنْتُمْ ظَالِمُوْنَ
You (dual) are magicians	أَنْتُمَا سَاحِرَانِ
I am an advisor	أَنَا نَاصِحٌ
I am successful	أَنَا فَائِزٌ
We are overpowring	نَحْنُ غَالِبُوْنَ
You are a believer	أَنْتَ مُؤْمِنٌ
You (f) are a believer	أَنْتِ مُؤْمِنَةٌ
They are polytheists	هُمْ مُشْرِكُوْنَ

They (f) are polytheists	هُنَّ مُشْرِكَاتٌ
I have conviction	أَنَا مُوْقِنٌ
We have conviction	نَحْنُ مُوْقِنُوْنَ
I have conviction (f)	أَنَا مُوْقِنَةٌ
We have conviction (f)	نَحْنُ مُوْقِنَاتٌ

Pronouns with Maf`ool

Singular

He requested him	طَلَبَهٗ
He requested them	طَلَبَهَا
He requested you	طَلَبَكَ
He requested you (f)	طَلَبَكِ
He requested me	طَلَبَنِيْ

Dual

He requested them	طَلَبَهُمَا
He requested them (f)	طَلَبَهُمَا
He requested you two	طَلَبَكُمَا
He requested you two (f)	طَلَبَكُمَا
He requested us	طَلَبَنَا

Plural

He requested them (m)	طَلَبَهُمْ
He requested them (f)	طَلَبَهُنَّ
He requested you (m)	طَلَبَكُمْ
He requested you (f)	طَلَبَكُنَّ
He requested us	طَلَبَنَا

LESSON SEVEN

Verbs

Past tense

Read	قَرَاَ	Spoke truthfully	صَدَقَ
Wrote	كَتَبَ	Disbelieved	كَفَرَ
Ate	أَكَلَ	Lied	كَذَبَ
Drank	شَرِبَ	Heard	سَمِعَ
Worshipped	عَبَدَ	Practised	عَمِلَ

Singular

He read   قَرَاَ

She read   قَرَاَتْ

You (m) read   قَرَاْتَ

You (f) read   قَرَاْتِ

I read   قَرَاْتُ

He wrote   كَتَبَ

She wrote   كَتَبَتْ

You (m) wrote   كَتَبْتَ

You (f) wrote   كَتَبْتِ

I wrote   كَتَبْتُ

He ate   أَكَلَ

She ate	اَكَلَتْ
You (m) ate	اَكَلْتَ
You (f) ate	اَكَلْتِ
I ate	اَكَلْتُ
He drank	شَرِبَ
She drank	شَرِبَتْ
You (m) drank	شَرِبْتَ
You (f) drank	شَرِبْتِ
I drank	شَرِبْتُ
He worshipped	عَبَدَ
She worshipped	عَبَدَتْ
You (m) worshipped	عَبَدْتَّ
You (f) worshipped	عَبَدْتِّ
I worshipped	عَبَدْتُ
He spoke truthfully	صَدَقَ
She spoke truthfully	صَدَقَتْ
You (m) spoke truthfully	صَدَقْتَ
You (f) spoke truthfully	صَدَقْتِ
I spoke truthfully	صَدَقْتُ
He disbelieved	كَفَرَ
She disbelieved	كَفَرَتْ
You (m) disbelieved	كَفَرْتَ

You (f) disbelieved	كَفَرْتِ
I disbelieved	كَفَرْتُ
He lied	كَذَبَ
She lied	كَذَبَتْ
You (m) lied	كَذَبْتَ
You (f) lied	كَذَبْتِ
I lied	كَذَبْتُ
He heard	سَمِعَ
She heard	سَمِعَتْ
You (m) heard	سَمِعْتَ
You (f) heard	سَمِعْتِ
I heard	سَمِعْتُ
He practised	عَمِلَ
She practised	عَمِلَتْ
You (m) practised	عَمِلْتَ
You (f) practised	عَمِلْتِ
I practised	عَمِلْتُ

Dual

They (m) read	قَرَءَا
They (f) read	قَرَءَتَا
You (m) read	قَرَئْتُمَا

You (f) rad	قَرَأْتُمَا
We read	قَرَأْنَا
They (m) wrote	كَتَبَا
They (f) wrote	كَتَبَتَا
You (m) wrote	كَتَبْتُمَا
You (f) wrote	كَتَبْتُمَا
We wrote	كَتَبْنَا
They ate (m)	أَكَلَا
They (f) ate	أَكَلَتَا
You (m) ate	أَكَلْتُمَا
You (f) ate	أَكَلْتُمَا
We ate	أَكَلْنَا
They (m) drank	شَرِبَا
They (f) drank	شَرِبَتَا
You (m) drank	شَرِبْتُمَا
You (f) drank	شَرِبْتُمَا
We drank	شَرِبْنَا
They (m) worshipped	عَبَدَا
They (f) worshipped	عَبَدَتَا
You (m) worshipped	عَبَدْتُمَا
You (f) worshipped	عَبَدْتُمَا
We worshipped	عَبَدْنَا

They spoke truthfully (m)	صَدَقَا
They spoke truthfully (f)	صَدَقَتَا
You (m) spoke truthfully	صَدَقْتُمَا
You (f) spoke truthfully	صَدَقْتُمَا
We spoke truthfully	صَدَقْنَا
They (m) disbelieved	كَفَرَا
They (f) disbelieved	كَفَرَتَا
You (m) disbelieved	كَفَرْتُمَا
You (f) disbelieved	كَفَرْتُمَا
We disbelieved	كَفَرْنَا
They (m) lied	كَذَبَا
They (f) lied	كَذَبَتَا
You (m) lied	كَذَبْتُمَا
You (f) lied	كَذَبْتُمَا
We lied	كَذَبْنَا
They (m) heard	سَمِعَا
They (f) heard	سَمِعَتَا
You (m) heard	سَمِعْتُمَا
You (f) heard	سَمِعْتُمَا
We heard	سَمِعْنَا
They (m) practised	عَمِلَا
They (f) practised	عَمِلَتَا

You (m) practised	عَمِلْتُمَا
You (f) practised	عَمِلْتُمَا
We practised	عَمِلْنَا

Plural

They read (m)	قَرَءُوْا
They read (f)	قَرَءْنَ
You read (m)	قَرَءْتُمْ
You read (f)	قَرَءْتُنَّ
We read	قَرَءْنَا
They (m) wrote	كَتَبُوْا
They (f) wrote	كَتَبْنَ
You (m) wrote	كَتَبْتُمْ
You (f) wrote	كَتَبْتُنَّ
We wrote	كَتَبْنَا
They (m) ate	اَكَلُوْا
They (f) ate	اَكَلْنَ
You (m) ate	اَكَلْتُمْ
You (f) ate	اَكَلْتُنَّ
We ate	اَكَلْنَا
They (m) drank	شَرِبُوْا
They (f) drank	شَرِبْنَ

You (m) drank	شَرِبْتُمْ
You (f) drank	شَرِبْتُنَّ
We drank	شَرِبْنَا
They (m) worshipped	عَبَدُوْا
They (f) worshipped	عَبَدْنَ
You (m) worshipped	عَبَدْتُمْ
You (f) worshipped	عَبَدْتُنَّ
We worshipped	عَبَدْنَا
They (m) spoke truthfully	صَدَقُوْا
They (f) spoke truthfully	صَدَقْنَ
You (m) spoke truthfully	صَدَقْتُمْ
You (f) spoke truthfully	صَدَقْتُنَّ
We spoke truthfully	صَدَقْنَا
They (m) disbelieved	كَفَرُوْا
They (f) disbelieved	كَفَرْنَ
You (m) disbelieved	كَفَرْتُمْ
You (f) disbelieved	كَفَرْتُنَّ
We disbelieved	كَفَرْنَا
They (m) lied	كَذَبُوْا
They (f) lied	كَذَبْنَ
You (m) lied	كَذَبْتُمْ
You (f) lied	كَذَبْتُنَّ

We lied	كَذَبْنَا
They (m) heard	سَمِعُوْا
They (f) heard	سَمِعْنَ
You (m) heard	سَمِعْتُمْ
You (f) heard	سَمِعْتُنَّ
We heard	سَمِعْنَا
They (m) practised	عَمِلُوْا
They (f) practised	عَمِلْنَ
You (m) practised	عَمِلْتُمْ
You (f) practised	عَمِلْتُنَّ
We practised	عَمِلْنَا

Note :

There are 14 forms of the past tense word. These should be practised abundantly so that the student can understand the sign of each properly and if they do not know the correct meaning, the next lesson should not be taught. The sign of the past tense is at the end of the word. Therefore, the last letter should be checked properly.

LESSON EIGHT

Mudaari` (Present and future tense)

He is reading or will read	يَقْرَءُ
He is speaking truthfully or will speak	يَصْدُقُ
He is lying or will lie	يَكْذِبُ
He is listening or will listen	يَسْمَعُ
He is making or will make	يَجْعَلُ
He understands or will understand	يَشْعُرُ

Singular

He is reading or will read	يَقْرَءُ
She is reading or will read	تَقْرَءُ
You (m) are reading or will read	تَقْرَءُ
You (f) are reading or will read	تَقْرَئِيْنَ
I am reading or will read	أَقْرَءُ
He is speaking the truth or will speak	يَصْدُقُ
She is speaking the truth or will speak	تَصْدُقُ
You (m) are speaking the truth or will speak	تَصْدُقُ
You (f) are speaking the truth or will speak	تَصْدُقِيْنَ
I am speaking the truth or will speak	أَصْدُقُ

He lies or will lie	يَكْذِبُ
She lies or will lie	تَكْذِبُ
You lie or will lie	تَكْذِبُ
You (f) lie or will lie	تَكْذِبِينَ
I lie or will lie	أَكْذِبُ
He listens or will listen	يَسْمَعُ
She listens or will listen	تَسْمَعُ
You listen or will listen	تَسْمَعُ
You (f) listen or will listen	تَسْمَعِينَ
I listen	أَسْمَعُ
He makes or will make	يَجْعَلُ
She makes or will make	تَجْعَلُ
You make or will make	تَجْعَلُ
You make or will make	تَجْعَلِينَ
I make or will make	أَجْعَلُ
He understands or will understand	يَشْعُرُ
She understands or will understand	تَشْعُرُ
You understand or will understand	تَشْعُرُ
You (f) understand or will understand	تَشْعُرِينَ
I understand or will understand	أَشْعُرُ

Dual

They (m) read or will read	يَقْرَاَنِ
They (f) read or will read	تَقْرَاَنِ
You (m) read or will read	تَقْرَاَنِ
You (f) read or will read	تَقْرَاَنِ
We read or will read	نَقْرَءُ
They (m) speak truthfully or will speak	يَصْدُقَانِ
They (f) speak truthfully or will speak	تَصْدُقَانِ
You (m) speak truthfully or will speak	تَصْدُقَانِ
You (f) speak truthfully or will speak	تَصْدُقَانِ
We speak truthfully or will speak	نَصْدُقُ
They lie or will lie	يَكْذِبَانِ
They (f) lie or will lie	تَكْذِبَانِ
You (m) lie or will lie	تَكْذِبَانِ
You (f) lies or will lie	تَكْذِبَانِ
We lie	نَكْذِبُ
They (m) listen or will listen	يَسْمَعَانِ
They (f) listen or will listen	تَسْمَعَانِ
You (m) listens or will listen	تَسْمَعَانِ
You (f) listens or will listen	تَسْمَعَانِ
listen or will listen	نَسْمَعُ
hey make or will make	يَجْعَلَانِ

They (f) make or will make	تَجْعَلَانِ
You (m) makes or will make	تَجْعَلَانِ
You (f) makes or will make	تَجْعَلَانِ
We make	نَجْعَلُ
They understand or will understand	يَشْعُرَانِ
They (f) understand or will understand	تَشْعُرَانِ
You (m) understand or will understand	تَشْعُرَانِ
You (f) understand or will understand	تَشْعُرَانِ
We understand	نَشْعُرُ

Plural

They read or will read	يَقْرَءُوْنَ
They (f) read or will read	يَقْرَأْنَ
You (m) read or will read	تَقْرَءُوْنَ
You (f) read or will read	تَقْرَأْنَ
We read	نَقْرَءُ
They speak truthfully or will speak	يَصْدُقُوْنَ
They speak truthfully or will speak	يَصْدُقْنَ
You (m) speak truthfully or will speak	تَصْدُقُوْنَ
You (f) speak truthfully or will speak	تَصْدُقْنَ
We speak truthfully or will speak	نَصْدُقُ
They lie or will lie	يَكْذِبُوْنَ

They (f) lie or will lie	يَكْذِبْنَ
You (m) lie or will lie	تَكْذِبُوْنَ
You (f) lie or will lie	تَكْذِبْنَ
We lie or will lie	نَكْذِبُ
They listen or will listen	يَسْمَعُوْنَ
They listen or will listen	يَسْمَعْنَ
You (m) listens or will listen	تَسْمَعُوْنَ
You (f) listens or will listen	تَسْمَعْنَ
We listen or will listen	نَسْمَعُ
They make or will make	يَجْعَلُوْنَ
They (f) make or will make	يَجْعَلْنَ
You (m) are making or will make	تَجْعَلُوْنَ
You (f) are making or will make	تَجْعَلْنَ
We are making or will make	نَجْعَلُ
They understand	يَشْعُرُوْنَ
They understand (f)	يَشْعُرْنَ
You understand	تَشْعُرُوْنَ
You understand (f)	تَشْعُرْنَ
We understand	نَشْعُرُ

Exercise

Make the Mudaari' form of all 14 words of the words below
and translate

He makes Sajdah or will make Sajdah   يَسْجُدُ

He understands or will understand   يَعْقِلُ

He knows or will know   يَعْلَمُ

He opens or will open   يَفْتَحُ

He believes or will believe   يُؤْمِنُ

He obeys or will obey   يُسْلِمُ

He reveals or will reveal   يُنَزِّلُ

He speaks the truth or will speak   يُصَدِّقُ

He lies or will lie   يُكَذِّبُ

He has conviction or will have conviction   يُوقِنُ

Note :

In order to recognize the Mudaari' form, the first and last letter
must be seen. When proper exercise is done and every student can
tell the forms and the translation, then the next lesson can be
studied.

LESSON NINE

Amr - Command

Make Sajdah (m)	اُسْجُدْ
You (plural) make Sajdah (m)	اُسْجُدُوْا
Make Sajdah (f)	اُسْجُدِیْ
You (plural) make Sajdah (f)	اُسْجُدْنَ
You worship (m)	اُعْبُدْ
You (plural) worship (m)	اُعْبُدُوْا
You worship	اُعْبُدِیْ
You worship (plural f)	اُعْبُدْنَ
Write (m)	اُكْتُبْ
Write (plural m)	اُكْتُبُوْا
Write (f)	اُكْتُبِیْ
Write (plural f)	اُكْتُبْنَ
Make ruku	اِرْكَعْ
Make ruku (plural m)	اِرْكَعُوْا
Make ruku (f)	اِرْكَعِیْ
Make ruku (plural f)	اِرْكَعْنَ
Drink	اِشْرَبْ
Drink (plural m)	اِشْرَبُوْا
Drink (f)	اِشْرَبِیْ

Drink (plural f)	اِشْرَبْنَ
Enter	أُدْخُلْ
Enter (plural m)	أُدْخُلُوْا
Enter	أُدْخُلِيْ
Enter (plural f)	أُدْخُلْنَ

Nahi - negative command

Do not make Sajdah (m)	لَا تَسْجُدْ
Do not make Sajdah (plural m)	لَا تَسْجُدُوْا
Do not make Sajdah (f)	لَا تَسْجُدِيْ
Do not make Sajdah (plural f)	لَا تَسْجُدْنَ
Do not worship (m)	لَا تَعْبُدْ
Do not worship (plural m)	لَا تَعْبُدُوْا
Do not worship (f)	لَا تَعْبُدِيْ
Do not worship (plural f)	لَا تَعْبُدْنَ
Do not make ruku' (m)	لَا تَرْكَعْ
Do not make ruku' (plural m)	لَا تَرْكَعُوْا
Do not make ruku' (f)	لَا تَرْكَعِيْ
Do not make ruku' (plural f)	لَا تَرْكَعْنَ
Do not write (m)	لَا تَكْتُبْ
Do not write (plural m)	لَا تَكْتُبُوْا
Do not write (f)	لَا تَكْتُبِيْ

Do not write (plural f)	لَا تَكْتُبْنَ
Do not drink (m)	لَا تَشْرَبْ
Do not drink (plural m)	لَا تَشْرَبُوْا
Do not drink (f)	لَا تَشْرَبِيْ
Do not drink (plural f)	لَا تَشْرَبْنَ
Do not enter (m)	لَا تَدْخُلْ
Do not enter (plural m)	لَا تَدْخُلُوْا
Do not enter (f)	لَا تَدْخُلِيْ
Do not enter (plural f)	لَا تَدْخُلْنَ

LESSON TEN

Joining words

Jaar and Majroor

Whichever word upon which a Jaar letter comes, the word after it will get kasrah. That word is called Majroor.

With	بِ	Angels	اَلْمَلَائِكَةُ
For	لِ	Book	اَلْكِتَابُ
By (for oath)	وَ	Aakhirah	اَلْآخِرَةُ
From	مِنْ	Jannah	اَلْجَنَّةُ
In	فِيْ	Jahannam	اَلنَّارُ
Upon	عَلَى	Time	اَلْعَصْرُ
Until	حَتَّى	Day	اَلنَّهَارُ
To	إِلَى	Night	اَللَّيْلُ
From	عَنْ	Forgiveness	مَغْفِرَةٌ
Like (for example)	كَ	Pebbles	حِجَارَةٌ
Allaah	اللهُ	Clay	سِجِّيْلٌ
Rasul	اَلرَّسُوْلُ		

With Allaah	بِاللهِ
for the Rasul	لِلرَّسُوْلِ
upon the angels	عَلَى الْمَلَائِكَةِ
from the book	مِنَ الْكِتَابِ
from the Aakhirah	عَنِ الْآخِرَةِ

In Jannah	فِى الْجَنَّةِ
To Jahannam	إِلَى النَّارِ
by the oath of time	وَالْعَصْرِ
In the day	فِى النَّهَارِ
To the night	إِلَى اللَّيْلِ
To forgiveness	إِلَى مَغْفِرَةٍ
Like a tree	كَشَجَرَةٍ
Upon the path	عَلَى صِرَاطٍ
From punishment	مِنْ عَذَابٍ
To the Masjid	إِلَى الْمَسْجِدِ
With the Rabb of mankind	بِرَبِّ النَّاسِ
From the Rabb of the universe	مِنْ رَبِّ الْعَلَمِيْنَ
In the chests of mankind	فِى صُدُوْرِ النَّاسِ
Like eaten straw	كَعَصْفٍ مَأْكُوْلٍ
From a painful punishment	مِنْ عَذَابٍ اَلِيْم
Upon the straight path	عَلَى صِرَاطٍ مُّسْتَقِيْمٍ
Like a good tree	كَشَجَرَةٍ طَيِّبَةٍ
From the green tree	مِنَ الشَّجَرِ الْأَخْضَرِ
With the people of the elephant	بِأَصْحَابِ الْفِيْلِ
With clay pebbles	بِحِجَارَةٍ مِّنْ سِجِّيْلٍ

Majroor with Pronoun

Singular

لَهُ	لَهَا	لَكَ	لَكِ	لِي
For him	For her	For you (m)	For you (f)	For me

Dual

لَهُمَا	لَهُمَا	لَكُمَا	لَكُمَا	لَنَا
For them (m)	For them (f)	For you (m)	For you (f)	For us

Plural

لَهُمْ	لَهُنَّ	لَكُمْ	لَكُنَّ	لَنَا
For them (m)	For them (f)	For you (m)	For you (f)	For us

Sentences

Sentences beginning with a noun

Overpowering	اَلْعَزِيْزُ
Wise	اَلْحَكِيْمُ
Very Merciful	رَؤُوْفٌ
Servants	اَلْعِبَادُ
Forgiver	اَلتَّوَّابُ
Successful	اَلْمُفْلِحُوْنَ
Follower	قَانِتُوْنَ
Obedient/submissive	مُسْلِمُوْنَ

Mubtada and Khabar

He is the Overpowering, the Wise	وَهُوَ الْعَزِيْزُ الْحَكِيْمُ
You are Overpowering, the Wise	اَنْتَ الْعَزِيْزُ الْحَكِيْمُ
Allaah is very Merciful to His servants	اَللهُ رَؤُوْفٌ بِالْعِبَادِ
That is better for you	ذَالِكُمْ خَيْرٌ لَّكُمْ
He is Forgiving, the Merciful	هُوَ التَّوَّابُ الرَّحِيْمُ
You see	اَنْتُمْ تَنْظُرُوْنَ
They know	هُمْ يَعْلَمُوْنَ
They are upon guidance	أُوْلَئِكَ عَلَى هُدًى
They are successful	أُوْلَئِكَ هُمُ الْمُفْلِحُوْنَ
They are all followers of Him	كُلٌّ لَّهُ قَانِتُوْنَ

We are submissive to Him	نَحْنُ لَهُ مُسْلِمُوْنَ
We worship Him	نَحْنُ لَهُ عَابِدُوْنَ
We are sincere for Him	نَحْنُ لَهُ مُخْلِصُوْنَ

Sentences beginning with a noun together with Huroof Mushaba be Fi`l

Pious people	اَلْأَبْرَارُ
One of bounty	نَعِيْمٌ
Evil people	اَلْفُجَّارُ
Jahannam	جَحِيْمٌ
What he intends	مَا يُرِيْدُ
Become Muttaqun	تَتَّقُوْنَ
Begin to understand	تَعْقِلُوْنَ
Become overpowering	تَغْلِبُوْنَ
You may heed the advice	تَذَكَّرُوْنَ
They may heed the advice	يَتَذَكَّرُوْنَ
They may be guided	يَهْتَدُوْنَ

Indeed Allaah is aware regarding him/it	إِنَّ اللّٰهَ بِهِ عَلِيْمٌ
Indeed you are definitely from the Mursaleen	إِنَّكَ لَمِنَ الْمُرْسَلِيْنَ
Indeed you are upon a straight path	إِنَّكَ لَعَلٰى صِرَاطٍ مُّسْتَقِيْمٍ
Indeed the pious will definitely be in bounty	إِنَّ الْأَبْرَارَ لَفِيْ نَعِيْمٍ

Indeed the evil will definitely be in jahannam	اِنَّ الْفُجَّارَ لَفِيْ جَحِيْمٍ
Indeed it is guidance and mercy	اِنَّهُ لَهُدًى وَّرَحْمَةً
But Allaah does what He intends	لٰكِنَّ اللهَ يَفْعَلُ مَا يُرِيْدُ
So that you may acquire taqwa	لَعَلَّكُمْ تَتَّقُوْنَ
So that you may understand	لَعَلَّكُمْ تَعْقِلُوْنَ
So that you may be grateful	لَعَلَّكُمْ تَشْكُرُوْنَ
So that you may be overpowering	لَعَلَّكُمْ تَغْلِبُوْنَ
So that you may heed advice	لَعَلَّكُمْ تَذَكَّرُوْنَ
So that they may heed advice	لَعَلَّهُمْ يَتَذَكَّرُوْنَ
So that they may be guided	لَعَلَّهُمْ يَهْتَدُوْنَ

Af'aal Naaqisah

Is	كَانَ	The best nation	خَيْرَ أُمَّةٍ
Those who hear	سَمِيْعًا	You have become	أَصْبَحْتُمْ
One who encompasses	مُحِيْطًا	Brothers	إِخْوَانًا
Those who testify	شُهَدَاءَ	A good example	أُسْوَةٌ حَسَنَةٌ
Witness	شَهِيْدًا	Do not become	وَلَا تَكُوْنُوْا
You be	كُنْتُمْ		

Allaah listens and sees	كَانَ اللهُ سَمِيْعًا بَصِيْرًا
Allaah is All Aware, Wise	كَانَ اللهُ عَلِيْمًا حَكِيْمًا
Allaah has knowledge of everything	كَانَ اللهُ بِكُلِّ شَيْءٍ عَلِيْمًا

Allaah encompasses everything   كَانَ اللهُ بِكُلِّ شَيْءٍ مُحِيْطًا

So that you may be witness upon the people   تَكُوْنُوْا شُهَدَآءَ عَلَى النَّاسِ

So that the Rasul may be a witness upon you   كُوْنَ الرَّسُوْلُ عَلَيْكُمْ

شَهِيْدًا

You are the best of nations   كُنْتُمْ خَيْرَ أُمَّةٍ

So that you may become brothers by the bounty of Allaah -

أَصْبَحْتُمْ بِنِعْمَتِهِ اِخْوَانًا

Verily there is in the Rasul of Allah a good example for you -

لَقَدْ كَانَ لَكُمْ فِيْ رَسُوْلِ اللهِ أُسْوَةٌ حَسَنَةٌ

Sentences beginning with a verb

Past tense

Placed a seal	خَتَمَ
Their hearts	قُلُوْبِهِمْ
Met	لَقُوْا
Believed	آمَنُوْا
They said	قَالُوْا
We have believed	آمَنَّا
Took	ذَهَبَ
Left them	تَرَكَهُمْ
Darkness	ظُلُمَاتٍ
Made	جَعَلَ
A carpet	فِرَاشًا
Roof	بِنَاءً
Created	خَلَقَ
Whatever is in the earth	مَا فِي الْأَرْضِ
Everything	جَمِيْعًا
Taught	عَلَّمَ
Rejected	أَبَى
Had pride	اِسْتَكْبَرَ
We have granted salvation	أَنْجَيْنَا

We made them drown	اَغْرَقْنَا
Family	آلَ
You have come to know	عَلِمْتُمْ
They went over the limit	اِعْتَدُوْا
We took	اَخَذْنَا
Your pledge	مِيْثَاقَكُمْ
We elevated	رَفَعْنَا
Above you	فَوْقَكُمْ
Mt. Toor	اَلطُّوْرَ

خَتَمَ اللهُ عَلَى قُلُوْبِهِمْ وَعَلَى سَمْعِهِمْ

Allaah placed a seal on their hearts and on their

اِذَا لَقُوا الَّذِيْنَ آمَنُوْا قَالُوْا آمَنَّا

When they meet those who believe, they say we believed

ذَهَبَ اللهُ بِنُوْرِهِمْ وَتَرَكَهُمْ فِيْ ظُلُمَاتٍ

Allaah took away their light and left them in darkness

جَعَلَ لَكُمُ الْأَرْضَ فِرَاشًا وَّالسَّمَاءَ بِنَآءً

He made the earth for you a carpet and the sky a roof

خَلَقَ لَكُمْ مَّا فِي الْأَرْضِ جَمِيْعًا

He created for you whatever is in the earth, everything

عَلَّمَ آدَمَ الْأَسْمَاءَ كُلَّهَا

Taught Aadam the names of everything

اَبٰى وَاسْتَكْبَرَ وَكَانَ مِنَ الْكٰفِرِيْنَ

He rejected and had pride and he was of the disbelievers

اَنْجَيْنَاكُمْ وَاَغْرَقْنَا آلَ فِرْعَوْنَ

We granted you salvation and we drowned the family of
Fir'awn

وَلَقَدْ عَلِمْتُمُ الَّذِيْنَ اعْتَدُوْا مِنْكُمْ

Verily you know those who transgressed the limits from
among you

وَاِذْ اَخَذْنَا مِيْثَاقَكُمْ وَرَفَعْنَا فَوْقَكُمُ الطُّوْرَ

When We took your pledge and elevated above
you Mt. Toor

Present and future tense

They believe	يُؤْمِنُوْنَ
In the unseen	بِالْغَيْبِ
They establish	يُقِيْمُوْنَ
From that which	مِمَّا
We have granted them as sustenance	رَزَقْنَا
They spend	يُنْفِقُوْنَ
They do	يَجْعَلُوْنَ
Their fingers	أَصَابِعَهُمْ
Their ears	آذَانِهِمْ
It is close	يَكَادُ
The lightning	اَلْبَرْقُ
Snatches	يَخْطَفُ
Their sight	أَبْصَارَهُمْ
Breaks	يَنْقُضُوْنَ
The promise of Allaah	عَهْدَ اللهِ
After making it firm	مِنْ بَعْدِ مِيْثَاقِهِ
Break	يَقْطَعُوْنَ
That it should be joined	أَنْ يُّوْصَلَ
They cause corruption	يُفْسِدُوْنَ
Do you make	أَتَجْعَلُ
Those	مَنْ

Cause corruption	يُفْسِدُ
Cause to flow	يَسْفِكُ
Blood	اَلدِّمَآءَ
We glorify	نُسَبِّحُ
Your praises	بِحَمْدِكَ
We mention purity	نُقَدِّسُ
That which you make apparent	مَا تُبْدُوْنَ
That which you hide	وَمَا كُنْتُمْ تَكْتُمُوْنَ

يُؤْمِنُوْنَ بِالْغَيْبِ وَيُقِيْمُوْنَ الصَّلَاةَ وَمِمَّا رَزَقْنَاهُمْ يُنفِقُوْنَ

They believe in the unseen and establish salaah
and spend of that which we have given them as sustenance

يَجْعَلُوْنَ أَصَابِعَهُمْ فِيْ آذَانِهِمْ

They place their fingers in their ears

يَكَادُ الْبَرْقُ يَخْطَفُ أَبْصَارَهُمْ

It is close that the lightning snatches their sight

فَيَعْلَمُوْنَ أَنَّهُ الْحَقُّ مِنْ رَّبِّهِمْ

So they will know that it was the truth from their Rabb

يَنْقُضُوْنَ عَهْدَ اللّٰهِ مِنْ بَعْدِ مِيْثَاقِهِ

They break the promise of Allaah after making it firm

وَيَقْطَعُوْنَ مَا أَمَرَ اللهُ بِهِ أَن يُوْصَلَ وَيُفْسِدُوْنَ فِي الأَرْضِ

And they break off that which Allaah commanded that
it be joined and cause corruption in the earth

أَتَجْعَلُ فِيْهَا مَن يُفْسِدُ فِيْهَا وَيَسْفِكُ الدِّمَآءَ وَنَحْنُ نُسَبِّحُ بِحَمْدِكَ
وَنُقَدِّسُ لَكَ قَالَ إِنِّي أَعْلَمُ مَا لاَ تَعْلَمُوْنَ
وَأَعْلَمُ مَا تُبْدُوْنَ وَمَا كُنتُمْ تَكْتُمُوْنَ

Do you make the one who causes corruption in it and
sheds blood and we mention Your praises and glorify You.
He said, 'indeed I know that which you do not know
and I know that which you make apparent and
that which you hide.'

Amr - Command

Guide us	اِهْدِنَا
The path	اَلصِّرَاطَ
Straight	اَلْمُسْتَقِيْمَ
Believe	آمِنُوْا
Call	اُدْعُوْا
Your witnesses	شُهَدَآءَ كُمْ
Besides Allaah	مِنْ دُوْنِ اللهِ
Give glad tidings	بَشِّرْ
They practised	عَمِلُوْا
Good	اَلصَّالِحَاتِ
Tell me	اَنْبِئُوْنِيْ بِاَسْمَآءِ هٰؤُلَآءِ
The names of all	بِاَسْمَآءِ هٰؤُلَآءِ
Tell them	اَنْبِئْهُمْ
Stay you	اُسْكُنْ
Your spouse	زَوْجُكَ
Both of you eat	كُلَا
With satiation	رَغَدًا
Wherever	حَيْثُ
Both of you want	شِئْتُمَا
Come down you	اِهْبِطُوْا
Enemy	عَدُوٌّ

Remember	اُذْكُرُوْا
My bounty	نِعْمَتِيَ
I granted you bounty	أَنْعَمْتُ
Fulfil	أَوْفُوْا
My promise	بِعَهْدِيْ
I shall complete	أُوْفِ

اِهْدِنَا الصِّرَاطَ الْمُسْتَقِيْمَ

Guide us to the straight path

اٰمِنُوْا كَمَآ اٰمَنَ النَّاسُ

Believe as the people have believed

اُعْبُدُوْا رَبَّكُمُ الَّذِيْ خَلَقَكُمْ

Worship your Rabb who created you

اُدْعُوْا شُهَدَآءَكُمْ مِنْ دُوْنِ اللهِ

Call your witnesses besides Allaah

بَشِّرِ الَّذِيْنَ اٰمَنُوْا وَعَمِلُوا الصَّالِحَاتِ

Give glad tidings to those who believe and do good deeds

اَنْبِئُوْنِيْ بِأَسْمَاءِ هٰؤُلَآءِ

Tell me the names of these things

يَا اٰدَمُ اَنْبِئْهُمْ بِأَسْمَآئِهِمْ

O Aadam, tell them the names of them

يَا آدَمُ اسْكُنْ أَنْتَ وَزَوْجُكَ الْجَنَّةَ

O Aadam, you and your spouse live in Jannah

وَكُلَا مِنْهَا رَغَدًا حَيْثُ شِئْتُمَا

And both of you eat from it to satiation
from wherever you want

اِهْبِطُوا بَعْضُكُمْ لِبَعْضٍ عَدُوٌّ

Come down some of you enemies of others

اذْكُرُوا نِعْمَتِيَ الَّتِيْ أَنْعَمْتُ عَلَيْكُمْ وَأَوْفُوْا بِعَهْدِيْ أُوْفِ بِعَهْدِكُمْ

Remember My bounty which I bestowed on youand fulfil
My promise, I shall fulfil your promise

أَقِيْمُوا الصَّلَاةَ وَآتُوا الزَّكٰوةَ

Establish Salaah and give Zakaat

Nahi - negative command

Do not make	لَا تَجْعَلُوْا
Partners	أَنْدَادًا
Do not go close	لَا تَقْرَبَا
You both will become	فَتَكُوْنَا
From the oppressors	مِنَ الظَّالِمِيْنَ
Do not buy	لَا تَشْتَرُوْا
A small price	ثَمَنًا قَلِيْلًا
Do not mix	لَا تَلْبِسُوْا
Do not search	لَا تَبْغِ
Do not eat	لَا تَأْكُلُوْا
Do not become despondent	لَا تَقْنَطُوْا
Do not move	لَا تَعْثَوْا
Do not place	لَا تُلْقُوْا
Your hands	بِأَيْدِيْكُمْ
To destruction	إِلَى التَّهْلُكَةِ
Do not make	لَا تَتَّخِذُوْا
A joke	هُزُوًا

لَا تَجْعَلُوْا لِلّٰهِ أَنْدَادًا وَّ أَنْتُمْ تَعْلَمُوْنَ

Do not make partners unto Allaah when you know

لَا تَقْرَبَا هٰذِهِ الشَّجَرَةَ فَتَكُوْنَا مِنَ الظَّالِمِيْنَ

Do not go close to this tree, for then you would be
of the mis-placers-oppressors

لَا تَكُوْنُوْا اَوَّلَ كَافِرٍ بِهِ

Do not be the first of the disbelievers in it

وَلَا تَشْتَرُوْا بِآيَاتِيْ ثَمَنًا قَلِيْلًا

Do not buy my verses for a small price

لَا تَلْبِسُوا الْحَقَّ بِالْبَاطِلِ

Do not mix the truth with falsehood

لَا تَبْغِ الْفَسَادَ فِي الْاَرْضِ

Do not seek corruption in the earth

لَا تَأْكُلُوْا اَمْوَالَكُمْ بَيْنَكُمْ بِالْبَاطِلِ

Do not consume your wealth amongst you with falsehood

لَا تَقْنَطُوْا مِنْ رَحْمَةِ اللهِ

Do not be despondent of the mercy of Allaah

لَا تَعْثَوْا فِي الْاَرْضِ مُفْسِدِيْنَ

Do not move in the earth as corrupters

لَا تُلْقُوْا بِاَيْدِيْكُمْ اِلَى التَّهْلُكَةِ

Do not place your hands into destruction

وَلَا تَتَّخِذُوْآ آيَاتِ اللهِ هُزُوًا

Do not take the verses of Allaah as a joke

Qur`aanic teachings

Imaan

I seek protection with Allaah from Shaytaan the rejected one

أَعُوْذُ بِاللهِ مِنَ الشَّيْطَانِ الرَّجِيْمِ

In the name of Allaah, the Beneficent, the Merciful

بِسْمِ اللهِ الرَّحْمٰنِ الرَّحِيْمِ

O you who believe, believe in Allaah, and His Rasuls and the book revealed upon the Rasul and the book revealed before it

يَاأَيُّهَا الَّذِيْنَ آمَنُوْا اٰمِنُوْا بِاللهِ وَرَسُوْلِهِ وَالْكِتَابِ الَّذِيْ
نَزَّلَ عَلٰى رَسُوْلِهِ وَالْكِتَابِ الَّذِيْ أَنْزَلَ مِنْ قَبْلُ

He who disbelieves in Allaah and His angels and His books and His Rusul and the Day of Qiyaamat, he had indeed gone far astray

وَمَنْ يَّكْفُرْ بِاللهِ وَمَلَائِكَتِهِ وَكُتُبِهِ وَرُسُلِهِ وَالْيَوْمِ الْآخِرِ فَقَدْ ضَلَّ ضَلَالاً بَعِيْدَا

Do not fear and do not grieve, when will be raised if you are Mu'mineen

وَلَا تَخَافُوْا وَلَا تَحْزَنُوْا وَأَنْتُمُ الْأَعْلَوْنَ إِنْ كُنْتُمْ مُّؤْمِنِيْنَ

Imaan

He	هُوَ
Allaah	اَللهُ
Who	اَلَّذِيْ
No	لَا
Deity	اِلٰه
No deity	لَا اِلٰه
But	اِلَّا
He	هُوَ
He is Allaah, there is no deity but Him	هُوَ اللهُ الَّذِيْ لَا اِلٰهَ اِلَّا هُوَ
Aware	عَالِمٌ
Unseen	اَلْغَيْبِ
Aware of the unseen	عَالِمُ الْغَيْبِ
And seen	وَالشَّهَادَةِ
Aware of the unseen and seen	عَالِمُ الْغَيْبِ وَالشَّهَادَةِ

عَالِمُ الْغَيْبِ وَالشَّهَادَةِ هُوَ الرَّحْمٰنُ الرَّحِيْمُ

He is aware of the unseen and the seen, He is Beneficent, Most Merciful

King	اَلْمَلِكُ
Pure Being	اَلْقُدُّوْسُ
Free of faults	اَلسَّلَامُ

One Who gives peace	اَلْمُؤْمِنُ
One Who takes into His protection	اَلْمُهَيْمِنُ
Overpowering	اَلْعَزِيْزُ
Powerful	اَلْجَبَّارُ
Great	اَلْمُتَكَبِّرُ
Glorify	سُبْحَانَ
Glorifies Allaah	سُبْحَانَ اللهِ
From that which	عَمَّا
They ascribe as partners	يُشْرِكُوْنَ

هُوَ اللهُ الَّذِيْ لَا اِلٰهَ اِلَّا هُوَ الْمَلِكُ الْقُدُّوْسُ السَّلَامُ الْمُؤْمِنُ الْمُهَيْمِنُ
الْعَزِيْزُ الْجَبَّارُ الْمُتَكَبِّرُ سُبْحَانَ اللهِ عَمَّا يُشْرِكُوْنَ

He is Allaah, there is no deity but Him, the King, the Pure Being
Free of faults, One who give peace, One Who takes into Hi
protection, the Overpowering, the Powerful, the Great. Allaah i
Pure of all that they ascribe as partners to Him

The Creator	اَلْخَالِقُ
The Maker	اَلْبَارِئُ
The Fashioner	اَلْمُصَوِّرُ
For Him	لَهٗ
Names	اَلْأَسْمَاءُ
Beautiful	اَلْحُسْنٰى
Glorify	يُسَبِّحُ

Him	لَهُ
Whatever	مَا
In	فِيْ
heavens	اَلسَّمٰوَاتِ
In the heavens	فِي السَّمٰوَاتِ
Earth	اَلْأَرْضِ
Whatever is in the heavens and the earth	مَا فِي السَّمٰوَاتِ وَالْأَرْضِ
And He	وَهُوَ
Overpowering	اَلْعَزِيْزُ
Wise	اَلْحَكِيْمُ

هُوَ اللهُ الْخَالِقُ الْبَارِئُ الْمُصَوِّرُ لَهُ الْأَسْمَاءُ الْحُسْنٰى يُسَبِّحُ لَهُ مَا
فِي السَّمٰوَاتِ وَالْأَرْضِ وَهُوَ الْعَزِيْزُ الْحَكِيْمُ

He is Allaah, the Creator, the Maker, the Shaper, for Him are the beautiful names, everything that is in the heavens and the earth glorifies Him, He is the Overpowering, the Wise

Ambiyaa and Rasul

Indeed we	اِنَّا
Sent revelation	اَوْحَيْنَا
To you	اِلَيْكَ
Just as	كَمَا
To	اِلٰى
Nooh	نُوْحٍ
And the Nabis	وَالنَّبِيّٖنَ
From	مِنْ
After him	بَعْدِهٖ
From after him	مِنْ بَعْدِهٖ

اِنَّا اَوْحَيْنَا اِلَيْكَ كَمَا اَوْحَيْنَا اِلٰى نُوْحٍ وَالنَّبِيّٖنَ مِنْ بَعْدِهٖ

Indeed we sent revelation to you just as we sent revelation to Nooh and the Nabis after him

And we sent revelation	وَاَوْحَيْنَا
To	اِلٰى

Names of Ambiyaa`

اِبْرَاهِيْمَ ، اِسْمَاعِيْلَ ، اِسْحَاقَ ، يَعْقُوْبَ ، عِيْسٰى ، اَيُّوْبَ ، يُوْنُسَ ، هَارُوْنَ ، سُلَيْمَانَ ، دَاوُ

braaheem, Ismaa'eel, Ishaaq, Ya'qoob, Isa, Ayyub, Yunus, Iaroon, Sulayman, Dawood

Progeny	اَلْاَسْبَاطِ
And we gave	وَآتَيْنَا
The book Zaboor (to Dawud ﷺ)	زَبُوْرًا

وَاَوْحَيْنَا اِلٰى اِبْرَاهِيْمَ وَاِسْمَاعِيْلَ وَاِسْحَاقَ وَيَعْقُوْبَ وَالْاَسْبَاطِ وَعِيْسٰى
وَاَيُّوْبَ وَيُوْنُسَ وَهَارُوْنَ وَسُلَيْمَانَ اٰتَيْنَا دَاوُدَ زَبُوْرًا

And we sent revelation to Ibraaheem and Ismaa'eel and Ishaaq and Ya'qoob and his progeny and Isa and Ayyub and Yunus and Iaroon and Sulayman and we gave the Zaboor to Dawood

And the Rasuls	وَرُسُلًا
We have indeed mentioned them	قَدْ قَصَصْنٰهُمْ
Upon you	عَلَيْكَ
And many Rasuls	وَرُسُلًا
Not	لَمْ
Mentioned	نَقْصُصْ
Them	هُمْ
Upon you	عَلَيْكَ
Allaah spoke	وَكَلَّمَ اللهُ
Musa	مُوْسٰى

| Spoke well | تَكْلِيمًا |

وَرُسُلًا قَدْ قَصَصْنَهُمْ عَلَيْكَ مِنْ قَبْلُ وَرُسُلًا لَمْ نَقْصُصْهُمْ عَلَيْكَ
وَكَلَّمَ اللهُ مُوسَى تَكْلِيمًا

And many Rasuls, indeed we have mentioned them upon you
from before and many Rasuls we have not mentioned upon
you and Allaah spoke well to Musa

O Nabi	يَٰٓأَيُّهَا النَّبِيُّ
Indeed We	إِنَّا
Have sent you	أَرْسَلْنَٰكَ
Testifier	شَاهِدًا
And	وَ
Giver of glad tidings	مُبَشِّرًا
Warner	نَذِيرًا
Caller	دَاعِيًا
To Allaah	إِلَى اللهِ
By His command	بِإِذْنِهِ
And a lamp	وَسِرَاجًا
Bright	مُنِيرًا

يَٰٓأَيُّهَا النَّبِيُّ إِنَّا أَرْسَلْنَٰكَ شَاهِدًا وَمُبَشِّرًا وَنَذِيرًا وَدَاعِيًا إِلَى اللهِ بِإِذْنِهِ وَسِرَاجًا مُنِيرًا

O Nabi, indeed We have sent you as a testifier, giver of glad
tidings, and a warner and a caller to Allaah by His command and
bright lamp

Angels

Indeed	اِنَّ
Allaah	اَللَّهَ
Angels	مَلَائِكَةُ
And His angels	وَمَلَائِكَتَهُ
Send salutations	يُصَلُّوْنَ
Upon	عَلَى
Nabi ﷺ	اَلنَّبِيِّ
Upon Nabi ﷺ	عَلَى النَّبِيِّ
O you who	يَآأَيُّهَا الَّذِيْنَ
Believe	اٰمَنُوْا
Send salutations	صَلُّوْا
Upon him	عَلَيْهِ
And send peace	وَسَلِّمُوْا
Abundant peace	تَسْلِيْمًا

اَنَّ اللّٰهَ وَمَلَائِكَتَهُ يُصَلُّوْنَ عَلَى النَّبِيِّ يَآأَيُّهَا الَّذِيْنَ
اٰمَنُوْا صَلُّوْا عَلَيْهِ وَسَلِّمُوْا تَسْلِيْمًا

ndeed Allaah and His angels send salutations upon Nabi ﷺ .
 you who believe, send salutations and abundant peace upon

He	مَنْ
Is	كَانَ

Enemy	عَدُوًّا
For Allaah	لِلّٰهِ
And His angels	وَمَلٰئِكَتِهِ
And	وَ
Rusul	رُسُلِ
His	هِ
And his Rusul	وَرُسُلِهِ
Names of two angels	جِبْرِیْلَ وَ مِیْكَلَ
So	فَ
Indeed	اِنَّ
Enemy	عَدُوٌّ
For	لِ
Disbelievers	كَافِرِیْنَ
For the disbelievers	لِلْكَافِرِیْنَ

مَنْ كَانَ عَدُوًّا لِلّٰهِ وَمَلٰئِكَتِهِ وَرُسُلِهِ وَجِبْرِیْلَ وَمِیْكَلَ فَاِنَّ اللهَ عَدُوٌّ لِلْكٰفِرِیْنَ

He who is an enemy for Allaah and His angels and Rusul and Jibreel and Mika'eel so indeed Allaah is an enemy for the disbelievers

Books

And	وَ
Indeed	لَقَدْ
We sent	اَرْسَلْنَا
Names of two Rasuls	نُوْحًا وَّاِبْرَاهِيْمَ
We made	جَعَلْنَا
In	فِيْ
Progeny	ذُرِّيَّةِ
In	فِيْ
Both of their progeny	ذُرِّيَّتِهِمَا
Nubuwwah	اَلنُّبُوَّةَ
And the book	وَالْكِتٰبَ

وَلَقَدْ اَرْسَلْنَا نُوْحًا وَّاِبْرَاهِيْمَ وَجَعَلْنَا فِيْ ذُرِّيَّتِهِمَا النُّبُوَّةَ وَالْكِتٰبَ

And indeed we sent Nooh and Ibraaheem and we made in their progeny Nubuwah and the book

Then	ثُمَّ
We sent after	قَفَّيْنَا
Upon	عَلٰى
Footsteps	آثَارِهِمْ
Our Rusul	بِرُسُلِنَا

And we sent after	وَقَفَّيْنَا
Isa the son of Maryam	بِعِيسَى ابْنِ مَرْيَمَ
And	وَ
We gave him	آتَيْنَاهُ
The Injeel (name of book)	اَلْاِنْجِيْلَ

ثُمَّ قَفَّيْنَا عَلَى آثَارِهِمْ بِرُسُلِنَا وَقَفَّيْنَا بِعِيسَى ابْنِ مَرْيَمَ وَآتَيْنَاهُ الْاِنْجِيْلَ

Then we sent after in their footsteps our Rusul and we sen
thereafter Isa the son of Maryam and We gave him the injeel

Indeed We	إِنَّا
Revealed	أَنْزَلْنَا
Tauraat	اَلتَّوْرَاةَ
In it	فِيْهَا
Guidance	هُدًى
Light	وَنُوْرٌ

إِنَّا أَنْزَلْنَا التَّوْرَاةَ فِيْهَا هُدًى وَنُوْرٌ

Then we sent after in their footsteps our Rusul and we ser
thereafter Isa the son of Maryam and We gave him the injeel

| And we gave | وَ آتَيْنَا |
| Dawood (Rasul) | دَاوُدَ |

Zaboor (name of book)	زَبُوْرًا

وَ آتَيْنَا دَاوٗدَ زَبُوْرًا

And We gave the Zaboor to Dawood

And we revealed	وَنُنَزِّلُ
From the Qur`aan	مِنَ الْقُرْآنِ
That	مَا
He	هُوَ
Cure	شِفَاءٌ
And mercy	وَرَحْمَةٌ
For the believers	لِلْمُؤْمِنِيْنَ

وَنُنَزِّلُ مِنَ الْقُرْآنِ مَا هُوَ شِفَاءٌ وَرَحْمَةٌ لِّلْمُؤْمِنِيْنَ

And We revealed from the Qur'aan that which is a cure and mercy
for the believers

Taqdeer

If reaches them	اِنْ تُصِبْهُمْ
Good	حَسَنَةٌ
They say	يَقُوْلُوْا
What is	فَمَا
For these people	لِهَٰٓؤُلَآءِ الْقَوْم
It is not close	لَا يَكَادُوْنَ
Understand	يَفْقَهُوْنَ
Matter	حَدِيْثًا

اِنْ تُصِبْهُمْ حَسَنَةٌ يَقُوْلُوْا هٰذِهِ مِنْ عِنْدِ اللهِ وَاِنْ تُصِبْهُمْ سَيِّئَةٌ يَقُوْلُوْا هٰذِهِ مِنْ عِنْدِكَ قُلْ كُلٌّ مِّنْ عِنْدِ اللهِ فَمَالِهَٰٓؤُلَآءِ الْقَوْمِ لَا يَكَادُوْنَ يَفْقَهُوْنَ حَدِيْثًا

If goodness comes to them they say this is from Allaah and if ba◄
comes to them they say this is from you. Say everything is from
Allaah. What is the matter with the nation, it is not close that the
understand the matter.

The day of Qiyaamat

And	وَ
Blown	نُفِخَ
In the trumpet	فِى الصُّوْرِ
So	فَ
Become unconscious	صَعِقَ
Whoever	مَنْ
In the heavens	فِى السَّمٰوٰتِ
In the earth	فِى الْاَرْضِ
But	اِلَّا
Who Allaah wants	مَنْ شَآءَ اللهُ
Then	ثُمَّ يَنْظُرُوْنَ
Blown	نُفِخَ
In it	فِيْهِ
A second time	اُخْرٰى
So then	فَاِذَا
They	هُمْ
Standing	قِيَامٌ
Looking	يَنْظُرُوْنَ

وَنُفِخَ فِى الصُّوْرِ فَصَعِقَ مَنْ فِى السَّمٰوٰتِ وَمَنْ فِى الْاَرْضِ اِلَّا
مَنْ شَآءَ اللهُ ثُمَّ نُفِخَ فِيْهِ اُخْرٰى فَاِذَاهُمْ قِيَامٌ يَّنْظُرُوْنَ

And when the trumpet will be blown then whoever is in the heavens and the earth will fall unconscious but for those whom Allaah wants then it will be blown into again and they will be standing and looking

And	وَ
Shine	اَشْرَقَتْ
Earth	اَلْاَرْضُ
With	بِ
Light	نُوْرِ
Their Rabb	رَبِّهَا
The light of their Rabb	بِنُوْرِ رَبِّهَا
Placed	وُضِعَ
Book	اَلْكِتَابُ
And the Rasuls will be brounght	وَجَايْءَ بِالنَّبِيِّيْنَ
And testifiers	وَالشُّهَدَآءِ
And decision will be made	وَقُضِيَ
Between them	بَيْنَهُمْ
Truth	اَلْحَقِّ
And they	وَهُمْ
Will not be oppressed	لَا يُظْلَمُوْنَ

وَاَشْرَقَتِ الْاَرْضُ بِنُوْرِ رَبِّهَا وَوُضِعَ الْكِتَابُ وَجِائْءَ بِالنَّبِيِّيْنَ وَالشُّهَدَآءِ
وَقُضِيَ بَيْنَهُمْ بِالْحَقِّ وَهُمْ لَايُظْلَمُوْنَ

And the earth will shine with the light of their Rabb and the book will be placed and the Nabis will be brought and testifiers and decision will be made between them with truth and they will not be oppressed

And	وَ
Given completely	وُفِّيَتْ
Every person	كُلُّ نَفْسٍ
Whatever	مَا
They did	عَمِلَتْ
And He (Allaah)	وَهُوَ
Knows better	أَعْلَمُ
Regarding that which they do	بِمَا يَفْعَلُوْنَ

وَوُفِّيَتْ كُلُّ نَفْسٍ مَّا عَمِلَتْ وَهُوَ أَعْلَمُ بِمَا يَفْعَلُوْنَ

And every person will be given in full what they did and He knows best regarding that which they do

Islaam

Indeed	اِنَّ
Deen-Religion	اَلدِّيْنَ
By	عِنْدَ
Allaah	اللهِ
By Allaah	عِنْدِ اللهِ
Islaam	اَلْاِسْلَامُ

اِنَّ الدِّيْنَ عِنْدَ اللهِ الْاِسْلَامُ

Indeed Deen-religion by Allaah is Islaam

And he	وَمَنْ
Likes	يَبْتَغِ
Besides Islaam	غَيْرَ الْاِسْلَامِ
Deen-Religion	دِيْنًا
It will never be accepted	فَلَنْ يُّقْبَلَ
From him	مِنْهُ

وَمَنْ يَّبْتَغِ غَيْرَ الْاِسْلَامِ دِيْنًا فَلَنْ يُّقْبَلَ مِنْهُ

And he who likes a Deen-religion other than Islaam, it will
never be accepted from him

And he who	وَمَنْ
Turns away	يَرْغَبُ عَنْ

From the Deen-religion of Ibraaheem	عَنْ مِلَّةِ اِبْرَاهِيْمَ
But	اِلَّا
He who	مَنْ
Makes foolish	سَفِهَ
Himself	نَفْسَهُ
And indeed	وَلَقَدْ
We chose them	اِصْطَفَيْنَاهُ
In the world	فِي الدُّنْيَا
And indeed they	وَاِنَّهُ
In the Aakhirat	فِي الْآخِرَةِ
Will definitely be from the pious	لَمِنَ الصَّالِحِيْنَ

وَمَنْ يَرْغَبُ عَنْ مِلَّةِ اِبْرَاهِيْمَ اِلَّا مَنْ سَفِهَ نَفْسَهُ وَلَقَدْ اِصْطَفَيْنَاهُ فِي الدُّنْيَا
وَاِنَّهُ فِي الْآخِرَةِ لَمِنَ الصَّالِحِيْنَ

And he who turns away from the Deen-religion of Ibraaheem, but
he one who makes himself foolish and indeed we have chosen
im in the world and indeed in the Aakhirat will be from the pious

When	اِذْ
Said	قَالَ
To him	لَهُ
His Rabb	رَبُّهُ
Become subservient	اَسْلِمْ
I have become subservient	اَسْلَمْتُ

For	لِ
For the Rabb of the universe	لِرَبِّ الْعٰلَمِيْنَ

اِذْ قَالَ لَهُ رَبُّهُ اَسْلِمْ قَالَ اَسْلَمْتُ لِرَبِّ الْعٰلَمِيْنَ

When his Rabb said to him, become subservient, he said, 'I have submitted to the Rabb of the universe.'

And	وَ
Made a bequest	وَصّٰى
With him	بِهَا
Ibraaheem	اِبْرَاهِيْمَ
His sons	بَنِيْهِ
And Ya`qoob	وَيَعْقُوْبُ
O my sons	يٰبَنِيَّ
Indeed Allaah	اِنَّ اللهَ
Chose	اصْطَفٰى
For you	لَكُمْ
The Deen-religion of Islaam	الدِّيْنَ
So never die	فَلَا تَمُوْتُنَّ
But	اِلَّا
In the condition that you are Muslims	وَاَنْتُمْ مُسْلِمُوْنَ

وَوَصّٰى بِهَا اِبْرَاهِيْمَ بَنِيْهِ وَيَعْقُوْبُ يٰبَنِيَّ اِنَّ اللهَ اصْطَفٰى لَكُمُ الدِّيْنَ
فَلَا تَمُوْتُنَّ اِلَّا وَاَنْتُمْ مُسْلِمُوْنَ

And Ibraaheem made a bequest to his sons and Ya'qoob, 'o my sons, indeed Allaah has chosen the Deen-religion of Islaam for you so do not die but in the condition that you are Muslims.'

The book of Salaah

Wudhoo`

O you who believe	يَٰٓأَيُّهَا الَّذِيْنَ آمَنُوْا
When	إِذَا
You stand	قُمْتُمْ
For salaah	إِلَى الصَّلٰوةِ
Then wash	فَاغْسِلُوْا
Your faces	وُجُوْهَكُمْ
And your hands	وَأَيْدِيَكُمْ
To the elbows	إِلَى الْمَرَافِقِ
And make masah	وَامْسَحُوْا
Of your heads	بِرُؤُوْسِكُمْ
And your feet	وَأَرْجُلَكُمْ
Till the ankles	إِلَى الْكَعْبَيْنِ

يَٰٓأَيُّهَا الَّذِيْنَ آمَنُوْا إِذَا قُمْتُمْ إِلَى الصَّلٰوةِ فَاغْسِلُوْا وُجُوْهَكُمْ وَأَيْدِيَكُمْ إِلَى الْمَرَافِقِ
وَامْسَحُوْا بِرُؤُوْسِكُمْ وَأَرْجُلَكُمْ إِلَى الْكَعْبَيْنِ

O you who believe, when you stand for Salaah, then wash you
faces and your hands to the elbows and make masah of your head
and your feet till the ankles

Ghusl

And if you	وَاِنْ كُنْتُمْ
Are is janaabat	جُنُبًا
Then seek thorough purity	فَاطَّهَّرُوْا

وَاِنْ كُنْتُمْ جُنُبًا فَاطَّهَّرُوْا

And if you are in the state of janaabat, then seek thorough purity, i.e. make ghusl

Tayammum

And if you	وَاِنْ كُنْتُمْ
Ill	مَرْضٰی
Or	اَوْ
On journey	عَلٰی سَفَرٍ
Or came	اَوْ جَآءَ
One of you	اَحَدٌ مِّنْكُمْ
From relieving himself	مِّنَ الْغَآئِطِ
Or you touched	اَوْ لٰمَسْتُمُ
Women	النِّسَآءَ
Then you do not find	فَلَمْ تَجِدُوْا
Water	مَآءً
Then intend	فَتَيَمَّمُوْا
Sand	صَعِيْدًا
Pure	طَيِّبًا
So wipe	فَامْسَحُوْا
Your faces	بِوُجُوْهِكُمْ
And your hands with it	وَاَيْدِيْكُمْ مِّنْهُ

وَاِنْ كُنْتُمْ مَّرْضٰی اَوْ عَلٰی سَفَرٍ اَوْ جَآءَ اَحَدٌ مِّنْكُمْ مِّنَ الْغَآئِطِ اَوْ لٰمَسْتُمُ النِّسَآءَ
فَلَمْ تَجِدُوْا مَآءً فَتَيَمَّمُوْا صَعِيْدًا طَيِّبًا فَامْسَحُوْا
بِوُجُوْهِكُمْ وَاَيْدِيْكُمْ مِّنْهُ

And if any of you are ill or on journey or any of you comes from relieving himself or any of you touched women-his spouse then he did not find water, then intend pure sand and wipe your faces and hands with it

Salaah

O you who believe	يَاأَيُّهَا الَّذِينَ آمَنُوْا
Make ruku`	اِرْكَعُوْا
And make Sajdah	وَاسْجُدُوْا
And worship	وَاعْبُدُوْا
Your Rabb	رَبَّكُمْ
And do	وَافْعَلُوْا
Good/piety	اَلْخَيْرَ
So that you people	لَعَلَّكُمْ
May be successful	تُفْلِحُوْنَ

يَاأَيُّهَا الَّذِينَ آمَنُوْا ارْكَعُوْا وَاسْجُدُوْا وَاعْبُدُوْا رَبَّكُمْ وَافْعَلُوا الْخَيْرَ لَعَلَّكُمْ تُفْلِحُوْنَ

O you who believe, make ruku' and make Sajdah and worshi
your Rabb and do good so that you may be successful

And strive	وَجَاهِدُوْا
In the Deen-religion of Allaah	فِي اللهِ
According to the right of striving	حَقَّ جِهَادِهِ
He	هُوَ
Chose you	اِجْتَبَاكُمْ
He has not made	وَمَا جَعَلَ
Upon you	عَلَيْكُمْ
In Deen-religion	فِي الدِّيْنِ

And difficulty	مِنْ حَرَجٍ

وَجَاهِدُوْا فِي اللهِ حَقَّ جِهَادِهِ هُوَ اجْتَبَاكُمْ وَمَا جَعَلَ عَلَيْكُمْ فِي الدِّيْنِ مِنْ حَرَجٍ

And strive in the Deen-religion of Allaah according to the right of
striving, He chose you and has not made any difficulty upon you
in Deen-religion

Deen-Religion	مِلَّةَ
Your father	أَبِيْكُمْ
Ibraaheem	إِبْرَاهِيْمَ
He	هُوَ
Named you	سَمَّاكُمْ
Muslims	اَلْمُسْلِمِيْنَ
From before	مِنْ قَبْلُ
And in this	وَفِيْ هٰذَا
So that	لِيَكُوْنَ
Rasul	اَلرَّسُوْلُ
Witness	شَهِيْدًا
Upon you	عَلَيْكُمْ
And you become	وَتَكُوْنُوْا
Witness	شُهَدَاءَ
Upon people	عَلَى النَّاسِ

مِلَّةَ أَبِيكُمْ إِبْرَاهِيمَ هُوَ سَمَّاكُمُ الْمُسْلِمِينَ مِنْ قَبْلُ وَفِي هٰذَا لِيَكُونَ الرَّسُولُ

شَهِيدًا عَلَيْكُمْ وَتَكُونُوا شُهَدَآءَ عَلَى النَّاسِ

The Deen-religion of your father Ibraaheem, he named you Muslims from before and in this so that the Rasul can be witness upon you and you can be witness upon people

Establish	فَأَقِيمُوا
Salaah	اَلصَّلٰوةَ
And give Zakaat	وَآتُوا الزَّكٰوةَ
And hold firm	وَاعْتَصِمُوا
Allaah	بِاللّٰهِ
He is your patron	هُوَ مَوْلٰكُمْ
So good	فَنِعْمَ
Owner	اَلْمَوْلٰى
And good	وَنِعْمَ
Helper	اَلنَّصِيرُ

فَأَقِيمُوا الصَّلٰوةَ وَآتُوا الزَّكٰوةَ وَاعْتَصِمُوا بِاللّٰهِ هُوَ مَوْلٰكُمْ فَنِعْمَ الْمَوْلٰى وَنِعْمَ النَّصِيرُ

So establish Salaah and give Zakaat and hold firmly onto Allaah He is your patron, so what a good patron and what a good helper

And give Zakaat	وَآتُوا الزَّكوٰةَ
And give a loan to Allaah	وَاقْرِضُوا اللهَ
A good loan	قَرْضًا حَسَنًا
And whatever	وَمَا
You sent forth	تُقَدِّمُوا
For yourselves	لِاَنْفُسِكُمْ
From goodness	مِنْ خَيْرٍ
You will find it	تَجِدُوهُ
By Allaah	عِنْدَ اللهِ

وَآتُوا الزَّكوٰةَ وَاقْرِضُوا اللهَ قَرْضًا حَسَنًا وَمَا تُقَدِّمُوا لِاَنْفُسِكُمْ مِنْ خَيْرٍ تَجِدُوهُ عِنْدَ اللهِ

And give Zakaat and give a good loan to Allaah and whatever you send forth for yourselves from goodness you will find it by Allaah

And whatever	وَمَا
You gave	آتَيْتُمْ
From interest	مِنْ رِّبًوا
So that it may increase	لِيَرْبُوَا
In the wealth of people	فِيْ أَمْوَالِ النَّاسِ
It does not increase	فَلَا يَرْبُوْا
By Allaah	عِنْدَ اللهِ
And whatever you gave	وَمَا آتَيْتُمْ
From Zakaat	مِنْ زَكوٰةٍ

Intending	تُرِيْدُوْنَ
The countenance of Allaah	وَجْهَ اللهِ
So these people	فَأُولَئِكَ
They	هُمُ
Are the multipliers	اَلْمُضْعِفُوْنَ

وَمَآ آتَيْتُمْ مِّنْ رِّبًا لِّيَرْبُوَا۟ فِيۤ أَمْوَالِ النَّاسِ فَلَا يَرْبُوا۟ عِنْدَ اللهِ وَمَآ آتَيْتُمْ مِّنْ زَكَوةٍ تُرِيْدُوْنَ وَجْهَ اللهِ فَأُولَئِكَ هُمُ الْمُضْعِفُوْنَ

And whatever you gave of interest so that it may increase in the wealth of the people, it does not increase by Allaah and whatever you gave of Zakaat intending the countenance of Allaah, so these people are those who multiply

Indeed	إِنَّ
Those who believe	اَلَّذِيْنَ آمَنُوْا
And did	وَعَمِلُوا
Good	اَلصَّالِحَاتِ
And established	وَأَقَامُوا
Salaah	اَلصَّلَوةَ
And gave Zakaat	وَآتَوُا الزَّكَوةَ
For them	لَهُمْ
Their reward	أَجْرُهُمْ
By	عِنْدَ
Their Rabb	رَبِّهِمْ
And no fear	وَلَاخَوْفٌ

Upon them	عَلَيْهِمْ
Nor will they	وَلَا هُمْ
Be grieved	يَحْزَنُوْنَ

اِنَّ الَّذِيْنَ آمَنُوْا وَعَمِلُوا الصَّالِحَاتِ وَاَقَامُوا الصَّلٰوةَ وَاٰتَوُا الزَّكٰوةَ لَهُمْ اَجْرُهُمْ عِنْدَ رَبِّهِمْ وَلَا خَوْفٌ عَلَيْهِمْ وَلَا هُمْ يَحْزَنُوْنَ

ndeed those who believe and do good deeds and establish Salaah
nd give Zakaat, for them will be their reward by their Rabb and
here will be no fear upon them and they will not be grieved

Fasting

O you who believe	يايها الذين آمنوا
Made obligatory	كُتِبَ
Upon you	عَلَيْكُمْ
Fasting	اَلصِّيَامُ
Just as it was made obligatory	كَمَا كُتِبَ
On	عَلَى
Those people	اَلَّذِيْنَ
Before you	مِنْ قَبْلِكُمْ
So that you	لَعَلَّكُمْ
May become Muttaqi	تَتَّقُوْنَ

يَاأَيُّهَا الَّذِيْنَ آمَنُوْا كُتِبَ عَلَيْكُمُ الصِّيَامُ كَمَا كُتِبَ عَلَى الَّذِيْنَ مِنْ قَبْلِكُمْ لَعَلَّكُمْ تَتَّقُوْنَ

O you who believe, fasting has been made obligatory upon you just as it was made obligatory on those before you so that you may become Muttaqi

The month of Ramadhaan	شَهْرُ رَمَضَانَ
Which	اَلَّذِيْ
Revealed	أُنْزِلَ
In it	فِيْهِ
Qur`aan	اَلْقُرْآنُ
Guidance	هُدًى

For people	لِلنَّاسِ
And clear signs	وَبَيِّنٰتٍ
From guidance	مِنَ الْهُدٰى
And separating between truth and falsehood	وَالْفُرْقَانِ
So whoever	فَمَنْ
Is present	شَهِدَ
From you	مِنْكُمْ
In the month	اَلشَّهْرَ
He should fast	فَلْيَصُمْهُ

شَهْرُ رَمَضَانَ الَّذِيْ اُنْزِلَ فِيْهِ الْقُرْاٰنُ هُدًى لِّلنَّاسِ وَبَيِّنٰتٍ مِّنَ الْهُدٰى
وَالْفُرْقَانِ فَمَنْ شَهِدَ مِنْكُمُ الشَّهْرَ فَلْيَصُمْهُ

he month of Ramadhaan in which the Qur'aan was revealed,
uidance for people and clear signs from guidance and separating
etween truth and falsehood, so whoever is present from you in
ie month should fast

Hajj

Indeed	اِنَّ
First	اَوَّلَ
House	بَيْتٍ
Made	وُضِعَ
For people	لِلنَّاسِ
Definitely	لَ
Which	اَلَّذِيْ
In Makkah	بِبَكَّةَ
Blessed	مُبَارَكًا
And guidance	وَهُدًى
For the universe	لِلْعٰلَمِيْنَ
In it	فِيْهِ
Signs	اٰيَاتٌ
Clear	بَيِّنَاتٌ
Place of standing	مَقَامُ
The place of standing of Ibraaheem	مَقَامُ اِبْرَاهِيْمَ

اِنَّ اَوَّلَ بَيْتٍ وُضِعَ لِلنَّاسِ لَلَّذِيْ بِبَكَّةَ مُبَارَكًا وَهُدًى لِلْعٰلَمِيْنَ

فِيْهِ اٰيَاتٌ بَيِّنَاتٌ مَّقَامُ اِبْرَاهِيْمَ

Indeed the first house made for people is the one in Makka
blessed and guidance for the universe. In it are clear signs, th
place of standing of Ibraheem

And whoever	وَمَنْ
Enters it	دَخَلَهُ
Will be	كَانَ
At peace	آمِنًا
And for Allaah	وَلِلّٰهِ
Upon people	عَلَى النَّاسِ
Hajj of the Ka`bah	حِجُّ الْبَيْتِ
Whoever	مَنِ
Has ability	اسْتَطَاعَ
To it	إِلَيْهِ
Path	سَبِيلًا
And whoever	وَمَنْ
Rejects	كَفَرَ
So indeed Allaah	فَإِنَّ اللّٰهَ
Independent	غَنِيٌّ
Of the universe	عَنِ الْعَالَمِيْنَ

وَمَنْ دَخَلَهُ كَانَ آمِنًا وَلِلّٰهِ عَلَى النَّاسِ حِجُّ الْبَيْتِ مَنِ اسْتَطَاعَ إِلَيْهِ سَبِيلًا وَمَنْ كَفَرَ فَإِنَّ اللّٰهَ غَنِيٌّ عَنِ الْعَالَمِيْنَ

nd whoever enters is will be at peace and for Allaah upon the ople is Hajj of the Ka'bah, whoever has the ability to undertake e journey (path) and whoever rejects, then Allaah is dependent of the universe

Hajj	اَلْحَجُّ
Months	اَشْهُرٌ
Known	مَعْلُوْمَاتٌ
Known months	اَشْهُرٌ مَعْلُوْمَاتٌ
So Whoever	فَمَنْ
Intends	فَرَضَ
In these months	فِيْهِنَّ
Hajj	اَلْحَجَّ
He was not open before women	فَلَا رَفَثَ
Nor did he sin	وَلَا فُسُوْقَ
Nor did he argue	وَلَاجِدَالَ
In Hajj	فِي الْحَجِّ

اَلْحَجُّ اَشْهُرٌ مَعْلُوْمَاتٌ فَمَنْ فَرَضَ فِيْهِنَّ الْحَجَّ فَلَا رَفَثَ وَلَا فُسُوْقَ وَلَاجِدَالَ فِي الْحَجِّ

Hajj is in the known months, so he who intends in them the Hajj
and is not shameless and does not commit sin and does not argu
in Hajj

And whatever you do	وَمَا تَفْعَلُوْا
Of goodness	مِنْ خَيْرٍ
He knows it	يَّعْلَمْهُ

وَمَا تَفْعَلُوْا مِنْ خَيْرٍ يَّعْلَمْهُ اللهُ

And whatever good you do, Allaah knows of it

Commands

Created	خَلَقَ
Man	اَلْاِنْسَانَ
From a clot of blood	مِنْ عَلَقٍ
And your Rabb	وَرَبُّكَ
Is very Beneficent	اَلْاَكْرَمُ
Taught	عَلَّمَ
Through the pen	بِالْقَلَمِ
That which he did not know	مَا لَمْ يَعْلَمْ

اِقْرَأْ بِاسْمِ رَبِّكَ الَّذِىْ خَلَقَ خَلَقَ الْاِنْسَانَ مِنْ عَلَقٍ اِقْرَأْ وَرَبُّكَ الْاَكْرَمُ الَّذِىْ عَلَّمَ بِالْقَلَمِ عَلَّمَ الْاِنْسَانَ مَا لَمْ يَعْلَمْ

ead in the name of your Rabb Who created, created man from a lot of blood. Read and your Rabb is Most Beneficent, He Who aught by means of the pen, He taught man that which he did not now

So recite	فَاقْرَءُوْا
Whatever	مَا
Easy	تَيَسَّرَ
From the Qur`aan	مِنَ الْقُرْآنِ

فَاقْرَءُوْا مَا تَيَسَّرَ مِنَ الْقُرْآنِ

So recite whatever is easy of the Qur'aan

Recite	اُتْلُ
Whatever	مَا
Revealed	اُوْحِىَ
To you	اِلَيْكَ
From the book	مِنَ الْكِتَابِ
And establish	وَاَقِمْ
Salaah	الصَّلٰوةَ
Indeed	اِنَّ
Salaah	الصَّلٰوةَ
Stops	تَنْهٰى
From shamelessness	عَنِ الْفَحْشَاءِ
And evil	الْمُنْكَرِ

اُتْلُ مَآ اُوْحِىَ اِلَيْكَ مِنَ الْكِتَابِ وَاَقِمِ الصَّلٰوةَ اِنَّ الصَّلٰوةَ
تَنْهٰى عَنِ الْفَحْشَاءِ وَ الْمُنْكَرِ

Recite that which has been revealed to you from the book an
establish salaah, indeed Salaah stops from shamelessness and ev

O my son	يٰبُنَىَّ
Establish salaah	اَقِمِ الصَّلٰوةَ
And command	وَاْمُرْ
Good	بِالْمَعْرُوْفِ
And prevent	وَانْهَ

From evil	عَنِ الْمُنْكَرِ
And have patience	وَاصْبِرْ
Upon that	عَلَى مَا
Defficulty which comes to you	أَصَابَكَ

يٰبُنَيَّ أَقِمِ الصَّلٰوةَ وَأْمُرْ بِالْمَعْرُوْفِ وَانْهَ عَنِ الْمُنْكَرِ وَاصْبِرْ عَلَى مَآ أَصَابَكَ

) my son, establish Salaah and command good and forbid evil
nd be patient upon the difficulty that comes to you

And adopt moderation	وَاقْصِدْ
In your walking	فِيْ مَشْيِكَ
And lower	وَاغْضُضْ
Your voice	مِنْ صَوْتِكَ
Indeed	إِنَّ
The worst	أَنْكَرَ
Of voices	الْأَصْوَاتِ
The worst of voices	أَنْكَرَ الْأَصْوَاتِ
Is the braying of a donkey	لَصَوْتُ الْحَمِيْرِ

وَاقْصِدْ فِيْ مَشْيِكَ وَاغْضُضْ مِنْ صَوْتِكَ إِنَّ أَنْكَرَ الْأَصْوَاتِ لَصَوْتُ الْحَمِيْرِ

nd adopt moderation in your walking and lower your voice
deed the worst of voices is the braying of a donkey

O you who believe	يَأَيُّهَا الَّذِينَ آمَنُوا
Stay away	اِجْتَنِبُوا
Many	كَثِيرًا
Thoughts	مِنَ الظَّنِّ
Indeed	إِنَّ
Some thoughts	بَعْضَ الظَّنِّ
Are sinful	إِثْمٌ

يَأَيُّهَا الَّذِينَ آمَنُوا اجْتَنِبُوا كَثِيرًا مِنَ الظَّنِّ إِنَّ بَعْضَ الظَّنِّ إِثْمٌ

O you who believe, stay away from many thoughts, indeed some thoughts are sinful

And hold firmly	وَاعْتَصِمُوا
With/onto	بِ
Rope	حَبْلِ
The rope of Allaah	حَبْلِ اللهِ
All together	جَمِيعًا
And do not split into groups	وَلَا تَفَرَّقُوا

وَاعْتَصِمُوا بِحَبْلِ اللهِ جَمِيعًا وَلَا تَفَرَّقُوا

And hold firmly onto the rope of Allaah all together and do not split into groups

Only	اِنَّمَا
Believers	الْمُؤْمِنِيْنَ
Brothers	اِخْوَةٌ
So reconcile	فَاَصْلِحُوْا
Between your brothers	بَيْنَ اَخَوَيْكُمْ
And fear Allaah	وَاتَّقُوا اللّٰه
So that mercy may be shown to you	لَعَلَّكُمْ تُرْحَمُوْنَ

اِنَّمَا الْمُؤْمِنِيْنَ اِخْوَةٌ فَاَصْلِحُوْا بَيْنَ اَخَوَيْكُمْ وَاتَّقُوا اللّٰه لَعَلَّكُمْ تُرْحَمُوْنَ

The believers are only brothers so reconcile between your brothers and fear Allaah so that mercy may be shown to you

Worship Allaah	وَاعْبُدُوا اللّٰه
And do not ascribe partners	وَلَا تُشْرِكُوْا
With him	بِهٖ
Anything	شَيْئًا
And with parents	وَبِالْوَالِدَيْنِ
Goodness	اِحْسَانًا
And with relatives	وَبِذِي الْقُرْبٰى
And orphans	وَالْيَتٰمٰى
And destitute	وَالْمَسَاكِيْنِ
And with neighbours	وَالْجَارِ
Family	ذِي الْقُرْبٰى

And neighbours who are relatives	وَالْجَارِ ذِي الْقُرْبٰى
And neighbours who are strangers	وَالْجَارِ الْجُنُبِ
And companion	وَالصَّاحِبِ
At the side	بِالْجَنْبِ
And the traveller	وَابْنِ السَّبِيْلِ

وَاعْبُدُوا اللهَ وَلَا تُشْرِكُوْا بِهِ شَيْئًا وَّبِالْوَالِدَيْنِ اِحْسَانًا وَّبِذِي الْقُرْبٰى وَالْيَتٰمٰى وَالْمَسَاكِيْنِ
وَالْجَارِ ذِي الْقُرْبٰى وَالْجَارِ الْجُنُبِ وَالصَّاحِبِ بِالْجَنْبِ وَابْنِ السَّبِيْلِ

And worship Allaah and do not ascribe anything as partner to Him
and do good to parents and with relatives and the orphans and the
destitute and neighbours who are family and neighbours who are
strangers and the companion by the side and the traveller

O you who believe	يٰٓاَيُّهَا الَّذِيْنَ اٰمَنُوْا
Fear Allaah	اِتَّقُوا اللهَ
According to the right of His fear	حَقَّ تُقَاتِهٖ
And do not die	وَلَا تَمُوْتُنَّ
But	اِلَّا
In the condition that you are Muslims	وَاَنْتُمْ مُّسْلِمُوْنَ

يٰٓاَيُّهَا الَّذِيْنَ اٰمَنُوا اتَّقُوا اللهَ حَقَّ تُقَاتِهٖ وَلَا تَمُوْتُنَّ اِلَّا وَاَنْتُمْ مُّسْلِمُوْنَ

O you who believe, fear Allaah according to the right of fearing
Him and never die but in the condition that you are Muslims

Negative Commands

O my beloved son	يٰبُنَیَّ
Do not ascribe partners	لَا تُشْرِكْ
To Allaah	بِاللهِ
Indeed	اِنَّ
Polytheism	الشِّرْكَ
Definitely	لَ
Great oppression	ظُلْمٌ عَظِيْمٌ

يٰبُنَیَّ لَا تُشْرِكْ بِاللهِ اِنَّ الشِّرْكَ لَظُلْمٌ عَظِيْمٌ

O my beloved son, do not ascribe partners to Allaah, indeed polytheism is definitely great oppression

Do not say	وَلَا تَقُلْ
To both of them	لَهُمَا
Uff	أُفٍّ
And do not scold them	وَلَا تَنْهَرْهُمَا
And say	وَقُلْ
To both of them	لَهُمَا
Speech	قَوْلًا
Noble	كَرِيْمًا
Noble speech	قَوْلًا كَرِيْمًا

وَلَا تَقُلْ لَهُمَا أُفٍّ وَلَا تَنْهَرْهُمَا وَقُلْ لَهُمَا قَوْلًا كَرِيمًا

And do not say uff to them and do not scold them and speak to them with noble speech

And do not walk	وَلَا تَمْشِ
In the earth	فِي الْأَرْضِ
Haughtily	مَرَحًا
Indeed you	اِنَّكَ
Can never tear	لَنْ تَخْرِقَ
The earth	اَلْأَرْضَ
And you will never reach	وَلَنْ تَبْلُغَ
The mountains	اَلْجِبَالَ
In height	طُولًا

وَلَا تَمْشِ فِي الْأَرْضِ مَرَحًا اِنَّكَ لَنْ تَخْرِقَ الْأَرْضَ وَلَنْ تَبْلُغَ الْجِبَالَ طُولًا

And do not walk in the earth haughtily indeed you can never tear the earth and you can never reach the mountains in height

And do not spy	وَلَا تَجَسَّسُوا
And do not backbite	وَلَا يَغْتَبْ
Some of you	بَعْضُكُمْ
Others	بَعْضًا

وَلَا تَجَسَّسُوْا وَلَا يَغْتَب بَّعْضُكُم بَعْضًا

And do not spy and some of you should not backbite others

Do not mutually argue	وَلَا تَنَازَعُوْا
You will become cowardly	فَتَفْشَلُوْا
And will go	وَتَذْهَبَ
Your wind	رِيْحُكُمْ
Your wind will come out	تَذْهَبَ رِيْحُكُمْ
And have patience	وَاصْبِرُوْا
Indeed Allaah	إِنَّ اللهَ
With	مَعَ
Those who are patient	ٱلصَّابِرِيْنَ
With those who are Patient	مَعَ الصَّابِرِيْنَ

وَلَا تَنَازَعُوْا فَتَفْشَلُوْا وَتَذْهَبَ رِيْحُكُمْ وَاصْبِرُوْا إِنَّ اللهَ مَعَ الصَّابِرِيْنَ

nd do not mutually argue, you will become cowardly and your
ind will come out of you and have patience. Indeed Allaah is
ith those who are patient

Do not mock	لَا يَسْخَرْ
A nation	قَوْمٌ
Another nation	مِنْ قَوْمٍ
It is close	عَسَى

That they will be	اَنْ يَّكُوْنُوْا
Better	خَيْرًا
Than them	مِنْهُمْ
And not women	وَلَا نِسَآءٌ
From women	مِنْ نِّسَآءٍ
Possibly	عَسٰى
They will be	اَنْ يَّكُنَّ
Better	خَيْرًا
Than those women	مِنْهُنَّ

يٰٓاَيُّهَا الَّذِيْنَ اٰمَنُوْا لَا يَسْخَرْ قَوْمٌ مِّنْ قَوْمٍ عَسٰٓى اَنْ يَّكُوْنُوْا خَيْرًا مِّنْهُمْ
وَلَا نِسَآءٌ مِّنْ نِّسَآءٍ عَسٰٓى اَنْ يَّكُنَّ خَيْرًا مِّنْهُنَّ

O you who believe, a nation should not mock another nation, it i
close that they are better than them and women should not moc
other women, possibly they could be better than them

And do not take out faults	وَلَا تَلْمِزُوْا
Of your people	اَنْفُسَكُمْ
And do not place amongst yourselves	وَلَا تَنَابَزُوْا
In	بِ
Names	اَلْاَلْقَابِ
With names	بِالْاَلْقَابِ

وَلَا تَلْمِزُوْا اَنْفُسَكُمْ وَلَا تَنَابَزُوْا بِالْاَلْقَابِ

And do not take out faults among yourselves and do not give each
other names

And do not spoil	وَلَا تُصَعِّرْ
Your faces	خَدَّكَ
For people	لِلنَّاسِ
And do not walk	وَلَا تَمْشِ
In the earth	فِي الْاَرْضِ
Haughtily	مَرَحًا

وَلَا تُصَعِّرْ خَدَّكَ لِلنَّاسِ وَلَا تَمْشِ فِي الْاَرْضِ مَرَحًا

And do not spoil your faces for people and do not walk haughtily
in the earth

Do not take	لَا تَتَّخِذُوْا
My enemy	عَدُوِّيْ
And your enemy	وَعَدُوَّكُمْ
Friend	اَوْلِيَآءَ

يَاَيُّهَا الَّذِيْنَ اٰمَنُوْا لَا تَتَّخِذُوْا عَدُوِّيْ وَعَدُوَّكُمْ اَوْلِيَآءَ

you who believe, do not take My enemy and your enemy as
iends

Do not take	لَا تَتَّخِذُوا
Those	اَلَّذِيْنَ
Made	اِتَّخَذُوا
Your Deen	دِيْنَكُمْ
Mockery	هُزُوًا
And play	وَلَعِبًا
From those	مِنَ الَّذِيْنَ
Who were given the book	أُوْتُوا الْكِتَابَ
Before you	مِنْ قَبْلِكُمْ
And the disbelievers	وَالْكُفَّارَ
Friends	أَوْلِيَآءَ
And fear Allaah	وَاتَّقُوا اللّٰهَ
If	إِنْ
You are	كُنْتُمْ
Believers	مُؤْمِنِيْنَ

يَٰٓأَيُّهَا الَّذِيْنَ اٰمَنُوْا لَا تَتَّخِذُوا الَّذِيْنَ اتَّخَذُوْا دِيْنَكُمْ هُزُوًا وَّلَعِبًا مِّنَ الَّذِيْنَ أُوْتُوا الْكِتَابَ مِنْ قَبْلِكُمْ وَالْكُفَّارَ أَوْلِيَآءَ وَاتَّقُوا اللّٰهَ إِنْ كُنْتُمْ مُؤْمِنِيْنَ

O you who believe, do not take those who have taken your Dee to be mockery and play from among those who were given th book before you and the disbelievers as friends, and fear Allaah you are believers

Qur`aanic Examples

The example of Kalima Tayyibah

Have you not seen	اَلَمْ تَرَ
How	كَيْفَ
Allaah explained	ضَرَبَ اللّٰهُ
Example	مَثَلًا
Speech	كَلِمَةً
Good	طَيِّبَةً
Tree	شَجَرَةٍ
Its roots	اَصْلُهَا
Firm	ثَابِتٌ
Its branches	فَرْعُهَا
In the sky	فِي السَّمَاءِ
It brings	تُؤْتِيْ
Its fruit	اُكُلَهَا
At every time	كُلَّ حِيْنٍ
By command	بِاِذْنِ
Of its Rabb	رَبِّهَا
Allaah explains examples	يَضْرِبُ اللّٰهُ الْاَمْثَالَ
So that they	لَعَلَّهُمْ
May heed advice	يَتَذَكَّرُوْنَ

اَلَمْ تَرَ كَيْفَ ضَرَبَ اللهُ مَثَلًا كَلِمَةً طَيِّبَةً كَشَجَرَةٍ طَيِّبَةٍ أَصْلُهَا ثَابِتٌ وَّ فَرْعُهَا

فِي السَّمَآءِ تُؤْتِيْ أُكُلَهَا كُلَّ حِيْنٍ بِاِذْنِ رَبِّهَا وَ يَضْرِبُ اللهُ

الْاَمْثَالَ لِلنَّاسِ لَعَلَّهُمْ يَتَذَكَّرُوْنَ

Do you not see how Allaah explains an example of a good word
like a good tree, its roots are firm and its branches are in the sky, i
brings its fruit at every time by the command of its Rabb and
Allaah explains examples for the people so that they may heed the
advice

The example of evil speech

Evil speech	كَلِمَةٍ خَبِيْثَةٍ
Uprooted	أُجْتُثَّتْ
On top	فَوْقِ
Its place	قَرَارٍ

وَ مَثَلُ كَلِمَةٍ خَبِيْثَةٍ كَشَجَرَةٍ خَبِيْثَةٍ اجْتُثَّتْ مِنْ فَوْقِ الْاَرْضِ مَا لَهَا مِنْ قَرَارٍ

And the example of evil speech is like an evil tree uprooted fro
above the ground, it has no place of standing

The example of the monotheist and the polytheist

Explained	ضَرَبَ
A person	رَجُلًا
A number of partners	شُرَكَاءُ
Those who have enmity amongst themselves	مُتَشَاكِسُوْنَ
Complete	سَلَمًا
What	هَلْ
Are both equal	يَسْتَوِيَانِ
All praise	اَلْحَمْدُ
Most of them	اَكْثَرُهُمْ
Do not know	لَا يَعْلَمُوْنَ

ضَرَبَ اللّٰهُ مَثَلًا رَّجُلًا فِيْهِ شُرَكَاءُ مُتَشَاكِسُوْنَ وَ رَجُلًا سَلَمًا لِّرَجُلٍ هَلْ يَسْتَوِيَانِ مَثَلًا اَلْحَمْدُ لِلّٰهِ بَلْ اَكْثَرُهُمْ لَا يَعْلَمُوْنَ

llaah explained the example of a man who has many partners
ho have enmity amongst themselves and a man complete for a
an, are they equal in example, all praise is for Allaah, but most
them do not know

The example of evil speech

Whoever	مَنْ
Ascribes partners	يُشْرِكْ
It is as though	فَكَأَنَّمَا
Fell	خَرَّ
From the sky	مِنَ السَّمَاءِ
Snatches him	تَخْطَفُهُ
Birds	اَلطَّيْرُ
Throws	تَهْوِيْ
Wind	اَلرِّيْحُ
A far place	مَكَانٍ سَحِيْقٍ

مَنْ يُّشْرِكْ بِاللهِ فَكَأَنَّمَا خَرَّ مِنَ السَّمَاءِ فَتَخْطَفُهُ الطَّيْرُ
اَوْ تَهْوِيْ بِهِ الرِّيْحُ فِيْ مَكَانٍ سَحِيْقٍ

He who ascribes partners to Allaah it is as though he fell from the sky and the bird snatches him or the wind blows him away to a far place

The example of those who take those other than Allaah to fulfil needs

Example of those people	مَثَلُ الَّذِيْنَ
Who made	اِتَّخَذُوا
Besides Allaah	مِنْ دُوْنِ اللهِ
Helpers	أَوْلِيَاءَ
Spider	اَلْعَنْكَبُوْتِ
It made	اِتَّخَذَتْ
A house	بَيْتًا
And indeed the weakest of houses	وَإِنَّ أَوْهَنَ الْبُيُوْتِ
Is definitely the house of the spider	لَبَيْتُ الْعَنْكَبُوْتِ
Only if they knew	لَوْ كَانُوْا يَعْلَمُوْنَ

مَثَلُ الَّذِيْنَ اتَّخَذُوا مِنْ دُوْنِ اللهِ أَوْلِيَاءَ كَمَثَلِ الْعَنْكَبُوْتِ اتَّخَذَتْ بَيْتًا وَإِنَّ أَوْهَنَ الْبُيُوْتِ لَبَيْتُ الْعَنْكَبُوْتِ لَوْ كَانُوْا يَعْلَمُوْنَ

he example of those who take those other than Allaah as helpers like the example of the spider who made a house and indeed the eakest of houses is definitely the house of the spider, if only they new

The example of Rasulullaah ﷺ and his companions

Severe	أَشِدَّاءُ
Soft hearted	رُحَمَاءُ
Making ruku`	رُكَّعًا
Making sajdah	سُجَّدًا
Searching	يَبْتَغُونَ
Their sign	سِيمَاهُمْ
Sajdah	اَلسُّجُودِ
Farm	زَرْعٍ
Shoot	شَطْأَ
Made firm	آزَرَ
Became thick	اِسْتَغْلَظَ
Stem	سُوقِ
Seems good	يُعْجِبُ
Farmers	الزُّرَّاعَ
So that they may anger	لِيَغِيظَ
Disbelievers	اَلْكُفَّارَ

مُحَمَّدٌ رَسُولُ اللهِ وَالَّذِينَ مَعَهُ أَشِدَّاءُ عَلَى الْكُفَّارِ رُحَمَاءُ بَيْنَهُمْ تَرَاهُمْ رُكَّعًا سُجَّدًا يَبْتَغُونَ فَضْلًا مِّنَ اللهِ وَرِضْوَانًا سِيمَاهُمْ فِي وُجُوهِهِم مِّنْ أَثَرِ السُّجُودِ ذَلِكَ مَثَلُهُمْ فِي التَّوْرَاةِ وَمَثَلُهُمْ فِي الْإِنْجِيلِ كَزَرْعٍ أَخْرَجَ شَطْأَهُ فَآزَرَهُ فَاسْتَغْلَظَ فَاسْتَوَى عَلَى سُوقِهِ يُعْجِبُ الزُّرَّاعَ لِيَغِيظَ بِهِمُ الْكُفَّارَ

Muhammad is the Rasul of Allaah and those with him are severe upon the disbelievers merciful amongst themselves, you see them making ruku' making Sajdah searching for the grace from Allaah and His pleasure. Their sign is in their faces from the effect of Sajdah. This is their example in the Tauraat and their example in the injeel is like a crop that has taken out its shoot and became firm, then it becomes thick and stands on its stem, pleasing the farmers in order to make the disbelievers angry

Example of the scholar who does not practise

Loaded	حَمَّلُوا
Then	ثُمَّ
Did not carry	لَمْ يَحْمِلُوْهَا
Donkey	اَلْحِمَارِ
Loaded	يَحْمِلُ
Books	اَسْفَارًا

مَثَلُ الَّذِيْنَ حُمِّلُوا التَّوْرَاةَ ثُمَّ لَمْ يَحْمِلُوْهَا كَمَثَلِ الْحِمَارِ يَحْمِلُ اَسْفَارًا

The example of those who carried the Tauraat then did not carry it like the example of a donkey carrying books

Example of the worldly life

Know	اِعْلَمُوا
Only	أَنَّمَا
The worldly life	أَلْحَيوةُ الدُّنْيَا
Play	لَعِبٌ
Amusement	وَلَهُوٌ
Beauty	وَزِينَةٌ
Priding	وَتَفَاخُرٌ
Amongst yourselves	بَيْنَكُمْ
Searching for more	وَتَكَاثُرٌ
Rain	غَيْثٍ
Seem good	أَعْجَبَ
Disbelievers	أَلْكُفَّارَ
Vegetation	نَبَاتٌ
Harvest	يَهِيجُ
Yellow	مُصْفَرًّا
Left over eaten straw	حُطَامًا
Goods of deception	مَتَاعُ الْغُرُورِ

اِعْلَمُوٓا أَنَّمَا الْحَيوةُ الدُّنْيَا لَعِبٌ وَلَهُوٌ وَزِينَةٌ وَتَفَاخُرٌ بَيْنَكُمْ وَتَكَاثُرٌ فِي الْأَمْوَالِ وَالْأَوْلَادِ كَمَثَلِ غَيْثٍ أَعْجَبَ الْكُفَّارَ نَبَاتُهُ ثُمَّ يَهِيجُ فَتَرَاهُ مُصْفَرًّا ثُمَّ يَكُونُ حُطَامًا وَفِي الْآخِرَةِ عَذَابٌ شَدِيدٌ وَمَغْفِرَةٌ مِّنَ اللهِ وَرِضْوَانٌ وَمَا الْحَيوةُ الدُّنْيَآ إِلَّا مَتَاعُ الْغُرُورِ

Know that the life of the world is play and amusement and beauty and priding amongst yourselves and searching for more wealth and children. Like the example of rain that pleases the disbelievers, then it is harvested then you see it yellow then it becomes like left over eaten straw and in the Aakhirat there is severe punishment and forgiveness from Allaah and His pleasure and the life of the world is nothing but goods of deception

Example of charity in the path of Allaah

Spend	يُنْفِقُوْنَ
Grain	حَبَّةٍ
Grown	أَنْبَتَتْ
Seven	سَبْعَ
Ears	سَنَابِلَ
Ear	سُنْبُلَةٍ
100	مِائَةُ
Multiply	يُضَاعِفُ
For whom	لِمَنْ
Wants	يَشَآءُ
Expander	وَاسِعٌ

مَثَلُ الَّذِيْنَ يُنْفِقُوْنَ أَمْوَالَهُمْ فِيْ سَبِيْلِ اللهِ كَمَثَلِ حَبَّةٍ أَنْبَتَتْ سَبْعَ سَنَابِلَ فِيْ كُلِّ سُنْبُلَةٍ مِائَةُ حَبَّةٍ وَاللهُ يُضَاعِفُ لِمَنْ يَّشَاءُ وَاللهُ وَاسِعٌ عَلِيْمٌ

The example of those who spend their wealth in the path of Allaah is like the example of a grain that grew seven ears, in every ear there are 100 grains and Allaah multiplies for whoever He wants and Allaah is the Expander, the All Aware

Example of the locality that is disobedient to Allaah

Allaah explained an example	ضَرَبَ اللهُ مَثَلًا
A town	قَرْيَةً
That was in peace	كَانَتْ آمِنَةً
Tranquility	مُطْمَئِنَّةً
Used to come to them	يَأْتِيْهَا
Its sustenance	رِزْقُهَا
With ease	رَغَدًا
From every place	مِنْ كُلِّ مَكَانٍ
So they were ungrateful	فَكَفَرَتْ
For the bounties of Allaah	بِأَنْعُمِ اللهِ
So Allaah made them taste	فَأَذَاقَهَا اللهُ
Clothing	لِبَاسَ

Hunger	اَلْجُوْع
And fear	وَالْخَوْف
On account of that which they used to do	بِمَا كَانُوْا يَصْنَعُوْنَ

وَ ضَرَبَ اللهُ مَثَلًا قَرْيَةً كَانَتْ آمِنَةً مُطْمَئِنَّةً يَأْتِيْهَا رِزْقُهَا رَغَدًا مِّنْ كُلِّ مَكَانٍ فَكَفَرَتْ بِأَنْعُمِ اللهِ فَأَذَاقَهَا اللهُ لِبَاسَ الْجُوْعِ وَالْخَوْف بِمَا كَانُوْا يَصْنَعُوْنَ

Allaah explained an example of a town that was in peace and tranquillity its sustenance used to come to it with ease from every place so they were ungrateful for the bounties of Allaah so Allaah made them taste the clothing of hunger and fear on account of that which they used to do

Du`aa`s

O our Rabb	رَبَّنَا
Do not turn	لَا تُزِغْ
Our hearts	قُلُوبَنَا
After	بَعْدَ إِذْ
You have guided us	هَدَيْتَنَا
And grant us	وَهَبْ لَنَا
From your side	مِنْ لَدُنْكَ
Mercy	رَحْمَةً
Indeed you	إِنَّكَ
You	أَنْتَ
The Giver	أَلْوَهَّابُ

رَبَّنَا لَا تُزِغْ قُلُوبَنَا بَعْدَ إِذْ هَدَيْتَنَا وَهَبْ لَنَا مِنْ لَدُنْكَ رَحْمَةً إِنَّكَ أَنْتَ الْوَهَّابُ

O our Rabb, do not turn our hearts after You have guided us an
grant us from Your side mercy, indeed You are the Giver

O our Rabb	رَبَّنَا
Grant us	أتِنَا
In the world	فِي الدُّنْيَا
And in the Aakhirat	وَفِي الْآخِرَةِ
Goodness	حَسَنَةً
And save us	وَقِنَا

Punishment of the fire	عَذَابَ النَّارِ

رَبَّنَآ اٰتِنَا فِي الدُّنْيَا حَسَنَةً وَّفِي الْاٰخِرَةِ حَسَنَةً وَّقِنَا عَذَابَ النَّارِ

O our Rabb, grant us goodness in this world and goodness in the Aakhirat and save us from the punishment of the fire

You grant	هَبْ
Us	لَنَا
From our spouses	مِنْ أَزْوَاجِنَا
And our progeny	وَذُرِّيّٰتِنَا
Coolness	قُرَّةَ
Eyes	أَعْيُنٍ
And make us	وَاجْعَلْنَا
For the Muttaqeen	لِلْمُتَّقِيْنَ
Leaders	إِمَامًا

رَبَّنَا هَبْ لَنَا مِنْ أَزْوَاجِنَا وَذُرِّيّٰتِنَا قُرَّةَ أَعْيُنٍ وَّاجْعَلْنَا لِلْمُتَّقِيْنَ إِمَامًا

O our Rabb, grant us from our spouses and our children the coolness of our eyes and make us leaders for the Muttaqeen

O my Rabb	رَبِّ
Forgive	اِغْفِرْ
And have mercy	وَارْحَمْ
And	وَ

You	أَنْتَ
Are the best of those who show mercy	خَيْرُ الرَّاحِمِيْنَ

رَبِّ اغْفِرْ وَارْحَمْ وَ اَنْتَ خَيْرُ الرَّاحِمِيْنَ

O my Rabb, forgive and have mercy and You are the best of those who show mercy

Make me	اِجْعَلْنِيْ
An establisher	مُقِيْمَ
And from my children	وَمِنْ ذُرِّيَّتِيْ
And accept	وَتَقَبَّلْ
My du`aa`	دُعَاءِ

رَبِّ اجْعَلْنِيْ مُقِيْمَ الصَّلٰوةِ وَمِنْ ذُرِّيَّتِيْ رَبَّنَا وَتَقَبَّلْ دُعَآءِ

O my Rabb, make me an establisher of Salaah and from m progeny o our Rabb, and accept my du'aa'

Upon you	عَلَيْكَ
We rely	تَوَكَّلْنَا
And to you	وَاِلَيْكَ
We return	اَنَبْنَا
Rrturn	اَلْمَصِيْرُ
Do not make us	لَا تَجْعَلْنَا
Trial	فِتْنَةً

And forgive us	وَاغْفِرْلَنَا
Indeed you alone	اِنَّكَ اَنْتَ
Overpowering	اَلْعَزِيْزُ
Wise	اَلْحَكِيْمُ

رَبَّنَا عَلَيْكَ تَوَكَّلْنَا وَاِلَيْكَ اَنَبْنَا وَاِلَيْكَ الْمَصِيْرُ رَبَّنَا لَا تَجْعَلْنَا فِتْنَةً لِّلَّذِيْنَ كَفَرُوْا وَاغْفِرْلَنَا رَبَّنَا اِنَّكَ اَنْتَ الْعَزِيْزُ الْحَكِيْمُ

) our Rabb, upon You do we rely and to You we return and to You
ʒ the return o our Rabb, do not make us a trial for those who
isbelieved and forgive us indeed You alone are Overpowering,
ʌll Wise

Guide us	اِهْدِنَا
The straight path	اَلصِّرَاطَ الْمُسْتَقِيْمَ
The path of those	صِرَاطَ الَّذِيْنَ
You have favoured	اَنْعَمْتَ
Upon them	عَلَيْهِمْ
Not that of those upon whom is anger	غَيْرِ الْمَغْضُوْبِ عَلَيْهِمْ
Not of those who have gone astray	وَلَا الضَّالِّيْنَ

اِهْدِنَا الصِّرَاطَ الْمُسْتَقِيْمَ صِرَاطَ الَّذِيْنَ اَنْعَمْتَ عَلَيْهِمْ
غَيْرِ الْمَغْضُوْبِ عَلَيْهِمْ وَلَا الضَّالِّيْنَ

ʋuide us to the straight path, the path of those whom You have
ʉided, not the path of those upon whom is anger, nor of those
ʰho have gone astray

O our Rabb	رَبَّنَا
Forgive us	اغْفِرْلَنَا
Our sins	ذُنُوْبَنَا
And our overstepping	وَاِسْرَافَنَا
In our matters	فِيْ اَمْرِنَا
Make firm	ثَبِّتْ
Our feet	اَقْدَامَنَا
And help us	وَانْصُرْنَا
Upon the disbelieving nation	عَلَى الْقَوْمِ الْكٰفِرِيْنَ

رَبَّنَا اغْفِرْلَنَا ذُنُوْبَنَا وَاِسْرَافَنَا فِيْ اَمْرِنَا وَ ثَبِّتْ اَقْدَامَنَا وَانْصُرْنَا عَلَى الْقَوْمِ الْكٰفِرِيْنَ

O our Rabb, forgive our sins and our overstepping in our affair and make our feet firm and help us against the disbelieving nation

Accept	تَقَبَّلْ
From us	مِنَّا
Hearer	اَلسَّمِيْعُ
All Aware	اَلْعَلِيْمُ

رَبَّنَا تَقَبَّلْ مِنَّا اِنَّكَ اَنْتَ السَّمِيْعُ الْعَلِيْمُ

O our Rabb, accept from us indeed You are the Hearer the All Aware

All praise is due to Allaah Who guided us and we would not have been guided if Allaah did not guide us

اَلْحَمْدُ لِلّٰهِ الَّذِيْ هَدَانَا لِهٰذَا وَمَا كُنَّا لِنَهْتَدِىَ لَوْلَآ اَنْ هَدَانَا اللّٰهُ

Translation edited by

A.H.Elias (Mufti)

21st Ramadhaan 1433

11th August 2012

OUR PUBLICATIONS
Available on Amazon

Logic for Beginners
Translation of تيسير المنطق

The Creed of Imam Tahawi
Arabic with *English* & *Farsi* translation

Sharh Al-Aqeedah An-Nasafiyyah
English Translation

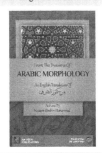

Solving Tarkeeb
Translation of حَلْ تَرْكِيب

Arabic Tutor: Arbi Ka Mu'allim
(Volumes 1, 2, 3, 4)

From the Treasures of Arabic
Morphology - من كنوز الصرف

Simplified Principles of Fiqh
Translation of آسان أصول فقہ

Miftah ul Qur'an
(Volumes 1, 2, 3, 4)

Masail Al Qudoori Made Easy
Question Answer Format (English)

Al-Hizbul A'zam
(Pocket Size)

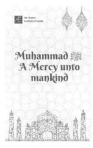

Tajweed for Beginners

Muhammad (SAW) -
A Mercy unto mankind

Etiquettes for Teachers
آداب المعلمين

Etiquettes for Students
آداب المتعلمين

Hadhrat Mufti Mahmood Hasan
Gangohi رحمة الله عليه

Hadhrat Moulana Maseehullah
Khan Saahib Sherwaani
رحمة الله عليه

The Life and Mission of Hadhrat
Moulana Husain Ahmad Madani
رحمة الله عليه

Hadhrat Moulana Muhammad
Qaasim Nanotwi رحمة الله عليه

Made in the USA
Monee, IL
13 February 2024